GREEN BARLEY

Essence

THE IDEAL "FAST FOOD"

GREEN BARLEY
Essence
THE IDEAL "FAST FOOD"

YOSHIHIDE HAGIWARA, M.D.

Adapted and Edited by
DOUG SMITH & DAN McTAGUE

Introduction by Richard A. Passwater, Ph.D.
Preface by William H. Lee, R.Ph.

Keats Publishing, Inc. New Canaan, Connecticut

Cover design concept: Atsuo Okawa

Green Barley Essence: The Ideal Fast Food is not intended as medical advice. Its intention is solely informational and educational. Please consult a medical or health professional should the need for one be warranted.

Library of Congress Cataloging in Publication Data

Hagiwara, Yoshihide, 1925–
    Young green barley essence.

    Translation of: Kyōi no kenkōgen bakuryokuso.
    1. Dried green barley juice—Therapeutic use.
2. Dried green barley juice.   I. Title.
RM666.B34H3413   1985   613.2′6   85-244
ISBN 0-87983-418-8

Printed in the United States of America

Published by Keats Publishing, Inc.
27 Pine Street (Box 876)
New Canaan, Connecticut 06840

Acknowledgments

I am honored at the publication of my book *Green Barley Essence*.

I am grateful to the editors at Keats Publishing, Inc. for their strong and sincere support and encouragement throughout the publishing of this book.

My thanks to Dr. Richard A. Passwater and Dr. William H. Lee for their introduction and preface.

I extend my appreciation to Doug Smith and Dan McTague, who devoted so much of their time to editing the original manuscript and adapting it to English. This book would not be here without their continuing and determined efforts.

Many thanks, particularly to Cheryl Hirsch, project editor at Keats Publishing, Inc. for her professional assistance and support.

Yoshihide Hagiwara, M.D.

ABOUT THE AUTHOR

Dr. Yoshihide Hagiwara has pursued three careers, as scientist, inventor and businessman. Born in 1925 in the Oita Prefecture of Japan and a graduate of Japan's Kumamoto University, Hagiwara began his first career as a young pharmacist devoted to the precepts of Western medicine. But Hagiwara's search for the right combination of manmade chemicals to cure man's ills came abruptly to an end with the discoveries of the human suffering caused by organic mercury. Seeing that the chemicals which were the subject of his research were part of the cause of man's suffering rather than the solution, Hagiwara turned his interest to the study of Chinese herb drugs and from there to nutrition. It was not long before his work focused upon the green barley plant, which he believed to be the richest source of nutrients on earth. Dr. Hagiwara developed a process to extract those nutrients into a green powder which he named *Bakuryokuso*, or *Green Barley Essence*. Today, that humble product is the basis of a multimillion-dollar health food industry in Japan that is now making its appearance in America, Europe and Australia.

EDITORS' NOTE

The manuscript upon which this book is based was written in Japanese by Dr. Hagiwara and has been published in its original version. The translated text was adapted for clarity and style in English.

Many of Dr. Hagiwara's assertions are bold and may provoke a reaction in the skeptical reader. Consideration should be given to the fact that the Japanese, through their experience with herbal and nutrient remedies dating to ancient times, are considerably more versed in this concept and better able to recognize its benefits than those raised in countries such as the United States where a strong tradition of surgical and chemical medicine prevails. Users of Green Barley Essence have reported remarkable improvement in their constitution and health. In this book, Dr. Hagiwara attempts to explain the reasons these results may occur. Dr. Hagiwara does not propose the use of Green Barley Essence as a treatment for any disease. He believes its regular use can significantly support the body's own health-promoting mechanisms. He welcomes and solicits any experiences or outside research which may help to establish the benefits and limitations of Green Barley Essence.

TABLE OF CONTENTS ▬▬▬

TABLES AND FIGURES

GREEN BARLEY ESSENCE
AT A GLANCE

CONTENTS BY VOLUME

Fiber	0.1 to 1.0%
Chlorophyll	0.9 to 1.5%
Protein	25.0 to 48.0%
Carbohydrates	23.0 to 40.0%
Fats (lipids)	1.5 to 4.5%

ACTIVE INGREDIENTS

Minerals	15.0 to 25.0%	See Table 2
Vitamins	Exceptional	See Table 3
Enzymes	20 identified	

CHEMICAL CHARACTERISTICS

Alkalinity	66.4 (higher than spinach)
Toxicity	None
Color	Deep green
Aroma	Mild to none
Taste	Raw green peas or green tea
Solubility (in water)	Instant
Absorbability (internally)	Excellent
Shelf life	Three Years
Dosage	One teaspoon 3 x day or more

METHOD OF CULTIVATION AND PROCESSING

Growing process	Organic
Herbicides	None used
Pesticides	None used
Chemical fertilizers	None used
Processing chemicals	None used
Processing temperature	Human body temperature
Preservatives	None used
Form	Powder or tablet

TABLE 1
Comparison of the Components of Various Foods and Green Barley Essence (%)

Food	Protein	Lipid	Carbohydrate
Green Barley Essence	**45.2%**	**3.2%**	**23.2%**
Milk (whole, fresh)	2.9%	3.3%	4.5%
Banana (raw)	1.3	0.4	21.4
Apple (raw)	0.4	0.5	10.4
Orange (raw)	0.8	3.3	9.3
Lettuce (raw)	1.0	0.2	2.4
Spinach (raw)	3.0	0.4	3.9
Tomato (raw)	1.3	0.3	6.9
Cabbage (raw)	1.6	0.2	2.4
Ice cream	4.0	8.5	21.8
Peanuts	26.3	48.2	17.0
Boiled rice	2.1	0.3	29.6

TABLE 2
Comparison of the Mineral Content of Green Barley Essence and Several Popular Foods (milligrams per 100 grams)

	Food	Na	K	Ca	Mg	Fe	Cu	P	Mn	Zn
	GREEN BARLEY ESSENCE	**775**	**8,880**	**1,108**	**224.7**	**15.8**	**1.36**	**594**	**5.6**	**7.33**
Vegetables	Celery	28	278	37	9.6	1.4	0.11	45	-	-
	Lettuce	30	208	21	9.7	0.5	0.15	25	-	-
	Spinach	25	490	98	59.2	3.3	0.26	52	-	-
	Onion	10	137	40	7.6	0.5	0.08	26	-	-
	Tomato	3	288	3	11.0	0.2	0.10	18	-	-
	Cabbage	15	240	45	16.8	0.4	-	22	-	-
	Kale	-	-	225	-	-	-	67	-	-
	Comfrey	19	-	-	-	9.0	-	40	-	-
Fruits	Banana	8	348	5	41.9	0.4	0.16	23	-	-
	Apple	8	-	3	-	0.2	-	7	-	-
	Orange	4	-	14	-	0.2	-	12	-	-
Grains	Wheat flour (wholegrain)	3	361	30	106.0	3.2	0.65	330	-	-
	Mixed wheat flour	3	132	118	34.1	1.9	0.17	111	-	-
	Refined rice (raw)	6	113	4	13.1	0.45	0.06	99	-	-
	Refined rice (cooked)	2	38	1	4.4	0.16	0.02	34	-	-
	Pressed barley	3	-	24	-	1.5	-	140	-	-
Dairy	Cow's milk	36	160	100	14.0	0.1	0.02	90	-	-
Fish	Salmon (canned)	500	320	170	29.8	1.2	0.05	320	-	-

Na: sodium
K: potassium
Ca: calcium
Mg: magnesium
Fe: iron
Cu: copper
P: phosphorus
Zn: zinc

TABLE 3
Comparison of the Vitamin Content of Green Barley Essence and Several Popular Foods

	Food	Carotene I.U.	B1 (mg)	B2 (mg)	B6 (mg)	C (mg)	E (mg)	H Biotin (µ)	Folic Acid (µ)	Pantothenic Acid*	Nicotinic Acid*	Chlorophyll (mg)	Choline (mg)
	Green Barley Essence	52,000	1.29	2.75	0.03	329	-	48.0	640	2.48	10.6	1490	260
Vegetables	Celery	0	1.03	1.02	0.10	10	0.5	0.1	7	0.40	0.4	-	-
	Lettuce	200	0.06	0.06	0.07	5	0.5	0.7	20	0.10	0.2	-	-
	Spinach	8,000	0.12	0.30	0.10	100	-	0.1	80	0.30	1.0	-	-
	Onion	20	0.03	0.02	0.10	10	0.3	0.9	10	0.10	0.2	-	-
	Tomato	400	0.08	0.03	0.10	20	0.4	1.2	5	0.05	0.8	-	-
	Cabbage	100	0.08	0.05	-	50	-	-	-	-	0.5	-	-
	Kale	10,000	0.15	0.33	-	126	-	-	-	-	-	-	-
	Comfrey	9,800	0.77	2.20	-	60	-	-	-	-	1.0	-	-
Fruits	Banana	200	0.03	0.05	0.30	10	0.4	-	10	0.20	0.5	-	-
	Apple	45	0.01	0.01	-	55	-	-	-	-	0.1	-	-
	Orange (fresh)	120	0.09	0.02	-	50	-	-	-	-	1.0	-	-
	Orange (concentrate)	20	-	-	-	3	-	-	-	-	1.0	-	-
Grains	Wheat flour	-	0.30	0.10	0.40	-	2.6	5.0	35	4.50	4.5	-	-
	Mixed wheat flour	-	-	-	0.10	-	1.7	0.6	14	0.80	-	-	-
	Refined rice (raw)	-	-	-	0.30	-	0.4	3.0	10	6.60	-	-	-
	Refined rice (cooked)	-	-	-	-	-	-	-	-	-	-	-	-
	Pressed barley	-	0.18	0.07	-	-	-	-	-	-	2.5	-	-
Dairy	Cow's Milk	20	0.04	0.15	0.04	2	-	2.0	0.3	0.35	-	-	-
Fish	Salmon (canned)	-	0.02	0.12	0.03	-	-	10.0	5.0	0.50	-	-	20.1

*milligrams

Presented by Resource Research Association, Office of Science and Technology, and Japan Food Analysis Center

SOME IDEAS ARE so simple and truthful that once they've been proposed we wonder why it took so long for them to be revealed.

That's one of the reasons this book has fascinated and intrigued me. The simple truth is that for 99 percent of the time man has lived on this earth he depended on the plant kingdom to supply all of the nutrients to keep him healthy and in good condition.

Our ancestors ate only raw foods and our digestive tract was designed to break down and convert those raw foods into living tissue. As time passed, man began to heat the harder parts of plants so they would become softer and easier to eat and "cooking" became part of our vocabulary. However, green plants were still the major part of our food supply.

It was not until the twentieth century that we have begun to mix chemical processing and food production, and it was not until we began to refine and process the nutrients out of our foods that "new" diseases began to appear. Diseases the world hadn't been aware of before. Diseases of the immune system; degenerative diseases such as hypertension, atherosclerosis, heart disease, arteriosclerosis; diseases brought about by heavy metals in the atmosphere and in the water and, of course, an increase in the incidence of cancer.

Doctor Yoshihide Hagiwara's own life experience led him to his eventual research into plant essences and to his conclusion that an extract of the nutritive factors derived from green leaves could serve as a food to promote health and maintain vitality. But first, it was his work as a research pharmacologist that led him to initial fame and fortune. Dr. Hagiwara was trained in modern pharmaceutical and medical techniques and used his remarkable talent to build a multimillion-dollar industry. However, he ignored his diet, and exposure to laboratory chemicals destroyed his health and part of his reasoning ability. When synthetic pharmaceuticals proved to be ineffective, he turned to two founding physicians of ancient times, Hippocrates, who stated: "A disease is to be cured naturally by man's own power, and physicians help it," and Shin-huang-ti who, in the Ch'in era of China said, "It is diet which maintains true health and becomes the best drug."

Dr. Hagiwara abandoned modern medicine, began a regimen that combined a natural diet with an assortment of Chinese herbs and recovered his health and mental agility. Along with the recovery came a deep conviction to pursue health in the pure natural products growing on God's good earth.

The story of his search for the most perfect single source of health, assisted by a dream which indicated that green leaves hold the secret, is the stuff of which legends are made.

Of course, without plants, life as we know it could not exist on Earth. Plants are the "lungs" of the planet, breathing out the oxygen all animal life needs to live. Plants are also the primary source of all that is of nutritional value.

When you consider the myriad of living plants, all green, all valuable, then consider all of their parts—

roots, stems, twigs, leaves and flowers—also, when is the best time to harvest, what should be in the soil to insure the finest quality and dozens of other variables, the task seems impossible.

Investigations over ten years slowly narrowed the field to a few of the most nutritious plants, but then other problems were encountered. Among them, taste!

Dr. Hagiwara's friends and relatives were subjected to countless "taste" contests. Chopped leaves, ground leaves, macerated leaves, leaves with stems attached, leaves without stems, leaves freshly harvested and leaves that had been standing in the sun. Dinner at the Hagiwaras' must have had a certain element of risk attached.

He finally discovered the combination of nutritive elements plus chlorophyll—the magic ingredient that enables plants to manufacture all of the food they need from carbon dioxide and sun energy—in the juice squeezed from the immature, embryonic leaves of the barley plant. However, that discovery began yet another search, this time for a method to prepare the juice for market without the loss of the valuable qualities.

How he solved the problems, the introduction of the product first to the Japanese market and now to the American market, his conclusions as to the benefits to health that may be expected when this product is used as a dietary supplement, make for a marvelous story.

You have only to walk into a modern supermarket and consider the amount of space devoted to selling fresh green vegetables. In most stores perhaps less than 10 percent of the space is fresh produce, the rest is stocked with processed foods, sugary cereals, canned foods, frozen foods, refined foods, etc. While most of us are aware of the need for fresh greens, we may find them hard to obtain. One answer is in this book!

William H. Lee, R.Ph.,

THE WESTERN WORLD is rediscovering some of the teachings and health products of the Eastern societies. Since the Japanese have the longest lifespans of any industrial nation, it is wise that we learn from them, adding the best of their knowledge to the best of our own, in particular taking the opportunity to study Japanese health foods and supplements to learn how we can benefit from them. This book describes the special nourishment of Green Barley Essence, but it also teaches the essence of the Japanese "natural food" philosophy which has contributed to the health of many Japanese and a few enlightened Americans.

As unlikely a food as "Green Barley Essence" sounds, it is a pleasant-tasting concentrate that restores to the average diet minerals, vitamins, amino acids and perhaps other food factors that have not yet been elucidated. Dr. Hagiwara is still researching several factors he believes to be present in young green barley leaves that may have special nutrient and even pharmacologic properties.

Of special interest in Dr. Hagiwara's research are the many enzymes in Green Barley Essence that may have protective properties if they are assimilated as he believes they are. Several scientists support the premise that these enzymes can be absorbed intact in sufficient quantities to be useful. Many scientists are also realizing that green vegetables have cancer-preventing properties due to food factors that are present in addition to their vitamin content. Yet most Americans do not eat sufficient quantities of green vegetables to produce optimum long-term health. However, Green Barley Essence is known to restore nutrients missing from many diets, and in addition, is suspected to have special protective factors.

The nutrient-rich Green Barley Essence can become a restorative that could replace the traditional chicken soup that Americans often rely on during colds or flus. Green Barley Essence is particularly rich in magnesium, potassium, beta-carotene, vitamin C and other minerals. The fact that nutrients, especially minerals, are easily absorbed by the body can explain much of the success attributed to Green Barley Essence. Trace minerals influence many enzymatic reactions in the body, yet the average diet contains less than optimal amounts of such minerals.

As mentioned earlier, Dr. Hagiwara believes that the key to the nutritive value of Green Barley Essence is not just the nutrient content of the concentrated extract, but its biochemical form, which promotes more effective assimilation. In connection with the matter of assimilation, Dr. Hagiwara points out a fact that may have great significance to us all, if it is confirmed by other studies—the effect on nutrients of freezing foods.

Most nutritionists regard freezing as a means of maintaining the nutritive value of foods. They feel that it preserves nutrients that are destroyed as fresh foods decay after being harvested. They overlook the scalding and other steps in the freezing process that destroy nutrients before the freezing occurs. While it is true that frozen foods will probably contain more useful nutrients than decayed foods, frozen foods should not be considered just as nourishing as fresh foods.

Now consider the new information introduced in this book by Dr. Hagiwara! "In Ireland one bleak winter, a spell of extremely cold weather was followed by a strange rash of paralysis in the limbs of sheep. Investigating the causes of the disease over the next several years, the British National Institute of Nutrition turned up evidence that implicated the frostbitten grasses upon which the sheep were feeding. An important mineral called molybdenum, when consumed in these grasses, could be absorbed into the sheep's bloodstream at only one-tenth the normal rate. The frost, it was learned, *converted molybdenum in the frozen grasses into a form extremely difficult to absorb*. Molybdenum, even in trace amounts, is essential to the body. Its deficiency caused malfunction of a specific enzyme which, in turn, induced leg paralysis."

Now, mind you, the grass wasn't deficient. No molybdenum was lost from the grass. It was only that the freezing process converted usable molybdenum into a virtually useless form that was poorly absorbed. The freezing was responsible for the deficiency. The grazing sheep continued to eat the grasses as if they were normal grasses. Nutritionists examining the grasses concluded after analysis that they contained all of the necessary nutrients in the normal amounts. Only after great study was it learned that a change had occurred to prevent the nutrients from being absorbed. Are we experiencing the same phenomenon? Are our bodies being fooled when we eat foods subjected to freezing?

Dr. Hagiwara explains. "In raw vegetables and meats, minerals are bonded in an organic form to enzymes, proteins, amino acids and sugars inside individual cells.

Scientifically, these are called organically bonded (chelated) minerals. But upon heating or freezing, silicic acid, phosphoric acid and other compounds intrude upon those mineral bonds, converting the minerals into an inorganic state which is not easily absorbed by man and (other) animals. It is as if the mineral were, in fact, removed from the food supply.

"Exactly the same process occurs when fresh farm produce is frozen in commercial plants to afford it long-term shelf life. Its mineral content is locked into a form that becomes inaccessible to the human system. The food may fill the stomach and satisfy the taste buds, but it will not nurture the body to a healthy state."

You can see that Dr. Hagiwara is warning us that our diets may be deficient because of poor food selection, foods grown in mineral depleted soil, and now a new concern—frozen foods with their meager minerals made largely unavailable to our bodies. Dr. Hagiwara is concerned that we add back these nutrients in a usable form—such as with Green Barley Essence—but I believe that further investigation of this problem is necessary, as well as restoring the nutrients.

Dr. Hagiwara presents several other new scientific concepts that need further discussion and study. They may all turn out to be important contributions to nutritional knowledge. He discusses potassium and energy, chlorophyll and blood and other concepts that make the book worth reading. There is much to be gained from this leading scientist from Japan in addition to learning about the advantages of Green Barley Essence.

Richard A. Passwater, Ph.D.

A FOOD FOR THE TWENTIETH CENTURY

DEEP GREEN LEAVES are the central site of creation in the lives of plants. In this book, I will offer the thesis that the creative power of these deep green leaves has always been the nutrient source of life and wellbeing for the human body as well, until the twentieth century disrupted the time-established wisdom of man's habits.

It is my belief that the steady depletion of that natural green power in the human diet, and its displacement by other nutrients of questionable value, constitutes the most serious threat of all to good health.

The threat follows two distinct paths, since, with the failure of our diet, we are letting our bodies fall apart from within, and at the same time they are subject to the greatest external attack that has ever been perpetrated on the health of man. Today the world is full of danger to our health, even in the foods we eat. Our bodies are being subjected to a direct external attack by pollutants, and, at the same time are affected internally by nutritional imbalance.

Illnesses are induced by an imbalance of minerals, enzymes and vitamins. Such imbalance can be caused directly, by the introduction of radiation, chemicals, inorganic drugs and other pollutants that are everywhere in the modern world. Or, it can be brought on indirectly by a deficiency in the diet. Most often, both causes act in combination.

While this book will focus primarily on the physical aspects of disease and nutrition, I should interject at the beginning that very often our less-than-perfect mental and emotional habits contribute substantially to the condition which allows physical imbalances in the body to occur. This becomes a vicious cycle as we come to rely more and more on technological processes to take the place of sound nutrition and sound mental attitudes about health.

The starting point in breaking this vicious cycle is to make a commitment to mental and physical habits which contribute to good health and the self-healing process. Beyond that, we must take advantage of the tools available to us to eliminate toxins from our bodies and to sustain the essential ingredients of life in their proper balance. I believe the best tool we have to accomplish both goals is a well-balanced nutrition program based upon the creative power of the green leaf.

This thesis became my incentive for an investigation covering more than ten years, during which I searched for a food that would promote health as well as maintain the vitality of the body. As I will tell shortly, I reached the conclusion that green juices of vegetables would best meet these requirements and that the best of these was the humble barley plant.

My work led to the development of a process to transform the power of the deep green leaf into a simple form which is easy to use, quite pleasant in taste and stable in form, without the use of preservatives, pesticides or artificial additives of any kind. I like to call it the "Ideal Fast Food" and I believe it can help rescue mankind from the poor state he has let himself fall into.

It may surprise you to learn that I found the source of that much-needed natural healing power in the agricultural fields of southern Japan where the barley plant presents a splendid cover of green. My research has shown that the green leaves of those barley plants contain the most prolific, balanced supply of nutrients that exists on Earth in a single source. Man himself cannot produce a better aid to health. My contribution has merely been to develop the means to cultivate, package and preserve those nutrients in a powder that is as easy to consume as a morning cup of coffee.

Simply stated, Green Barley Essence is an extract of the young leaves of barley or certain other cereal grasses such as rye and oats. Of these, the young leaves of rye contain the most active ingredients. The leaves of wheat are less attractive because of their small size and light green color. Yet, overall, the leaves of barley are best in quality. Most frequently used are the young leaves of a variety scientifically named *Hordeum Vulgare* 1 (*Nudum Hook Akashinriki* in Japanese). Green Barley Essence powders now on the market are made from this variety almost without exception.

In my experience, when used as a general tonic for the prevention of all diseases and to promote balance in the emotions and mind, Green Barley Essence is unsurpassed.

No doubt, thick green vegetables containing abundant natural vitamins, minerals and enzymes are essential in our daily diets. Green Barley Essence is the best among them. You may be interested to know, for example, that it is seven times richer in vitamin C than an equivalent weight of oranges and five times richer in iron than spinach. (More such comparisons are shown in Table 4.) Moreover, Green Barley Essence contains great amounts of natural chlorophyll, many enzymes used in human metabolism and substances which, research in my laboratory indicates, can inhibit the growth of cancer cells, activate living cells, and prevent the aging of cells. In addition, Green Barley Essence has a purifying effect which enables the body to eliminate many toxins that would otherwise accumulate, leading to disease.

TABLE 4
Amounts of Other Foods Required to Correspond to a Teaspoonful (3g) of Green Barley Essence

Nutrient	Milk (milliliters)	Lettuce (grams)	Tomato (grams)
Fats	3.0	50.0	32.0
Potassium	167.0	128.3	92.7
Calcium	33.3	158.6	1,110.0
Carotene (including vitamin A)	1,300.0	780.0	390.3
Vitamin B2	55.0	138.0	275.0
Vitamin C	492.3	200.0	49.2

More than fifteen years have elapsed since I became aware of the effects of Green Barley Essence, and during this time, I have frequently witnessed, in the hospitals of Japanese national universities, the successful treatment of diseases which are difficult to cure, such as leukemia, hypertension, atopic dermatitis, pancreatitis and peptic ulcer. In the area of preventive medicine, Green Barley Essence has proved to be effective against pimples, skin roughening, overweight and neurosis.

Unlike many solutions offered for the betterment of man's health, Green Barley Essence is not a fad remedy with a narrow focus. For too long we have been misled by "calorie dietetics," which stress high reliance on certain foods over others. Because of this thinking, we eat excessive quantities of acidic foods such as meat. At the same time, we rely too much upon processed foods for convenience. In contrast, Green Barley Essence is a pure natural food which provides the body with a wide range of the most-needed nutrients. Nothing has to be subtracted from the normal diet to receive its benefits and it can be taken in any quantity without fear of side effects.

Because of the success of this product in Japan since I introduced it in 1970, I brought it to America in 1980. The tremendous response it received encouraged me to write this book about Green Barley Essence telling of its great potential and my hope for the future health of mankind through the natural essences of nature's plants.

I would ask the indulgence of the more scientific reader. This book is not meant to be a scientific treatise, but merely a basic and general review of the modern world's approach to health. The burden lies with the scientific community to examine and prove or disprove these ideas. I am confident that such proof will be forthcoming.

Before I go on to a more detailed description of Green Barley Essence, let me interrupt the narrative briefly to relate the events that turned me in the direction of good health and, consequently, led to the discovery of Green Barley Essence. It is a personal story, the account of my own misguided efforts to brew good health in a chemical laboratory and the terrible price I paid.

I will tell my story briefly, because I think it shows how we have all gone astray in the quest for solutions where they cannot be found.

CHAPTER 1 ══════════════════════════

EPOCH OF DEGRADED HEALTH

MY OWN HEALTH GOES TO RUIN

I AM a research pharmacologist by training and, as is natural from that perspective, I once dedicated my life to the search for health in the world of drugs and chemicals. But I learned through bitter experience that drugs and chemicals are often not what they seem, leading only to an appearance of wellbeing, when in reality, they are corroding the very powers of health that are the natural inheritance of every one of us.

My lifelong interest in health must have been stimulated by my experiences as a child, when I knew disease in many forms. I can say now that, had I been more perceptive then, I might have saved myself and perhaps others in the world a lot of suffering from the effects of "chemical" solutions.

I was adopted at the age of seven by a family residing in Goto Islands, Nagasaki, because my natural father, a marine police officer, had stomach troubles and was compelled to stop working. My adopted father was a whaler, who sailed away for months at a time on expeditions to the Arctic Ocean. During one of his trips, when I was ten and in the fifth grade, my adopted mother fell

1

ill and began wasting away in bed. Out of necessity, I managed to learn to prepare boiled rice and soybean soup, and ate them day and night along with some pickles. I ate only that for six months.

One day, in a feeble voice, the woman sent me back to my own parents, saying there would be no hope for her recovery. Later, I understood that she was suffering from cancer of the womb. By then, I too was in poor health from the unbalanced nutrition I gleaned from my subsistence diet.

Shortly after I was home in my feeble and malnourished state, I caught a cold which developed into pulmonary hilar infiltration. This is generally regarded as a form of infantile tuberculosis. I stayed home from school for one year during my entire sixth grade.

I can see clearly now that my recovery from this illness was due to the positive physical exercises and the balanced diet I was given, which consisted of vegetables, potatoes, soybeans, millet grain, dried sardine and other healthful foods.

I was feeling "immortal" by the time I entered the university in 1945, and devoted myself to pharmacological studies.

After graduating from the Pharmaceutical Department of Kumamoto University, I ran a pharmacy in Oita, my native town, in order to support myself and my parents. Meanwhile, I wanted to devote every possible minute of the day to research work. At the end of each day I retired to a small room at my home to work far into the night, often until 4 or 5 o'clock in the morning. I followed this pattern for at least fifteen years, sleeping only three hours a day and spending the rest of my time in my laboratory.

My customers at this time often complained of the inadequacy of the medications for athlete's foot, so I concentrated my efforts on this affliction. About 1955, I produced an effective drug using an active ingredient extracted from garlic. Since its efficacy was unmatched, it quickly gained a reputation. To tell the truth, this drug contained mercury, although it was first manufactured before the epidemic of Minamata disease which was later discovered to be caused by organic mercury.

Unaware of its possible harmful effects, I built a business upon my new formula, which sold under the name **Alber**. I moved to Osaka, and founded my own pharmaceutical company for manufacturing and selling this drug. I still led the life of a research pharmacologist rather than just sitting at a desk as company president.

More successful products followed. The best were Shiden, a hair-nourishing preparation, and May Young, a luxurious facial cream, which are both still on the market. Shiden became a huge success immediately and generated $4 million in revenues.

My hard work seemed to have paid off. I was the owner of Yamashiro Pharmaceutical Co., Ltd., the largest drug maker in Japan. At its peak, Yamashiro employed 700 people. In all, it brought out more than 200 health products for women, for skin disease, kidney and stomach problems, high blood pressure, neurosis and stress. At that time, I felt and acted more energetic than ordinary people.

But my life was not going as smoothly as I thought. In 1963, organic mercury was banned from sale. I, who had been handling it for many years and experimenting with it upon myself, soon learned for myself the damage it causes. About that time, both my physical and mental strength suddenly began to fail. My teeth decayed and fell out because of alveolar pyorrhea. My hair turned gray when I was only thirty-eight years old. I lost the power, physically and mentally, to lead and supervise my staff.

— I made up my mind then to take decisive measures to regain my health. I took all kinds of vitamin tablets and concocted a shot of hormone preparations. I mixed 20 mg of Prehormone, a pituitary hormone, 20 mg of vitamin B1, 100 mg of vitamin C and glucose, and gave myself the injection. At one time, I even took a shot of a stimulant drug in an attempt to remove the heavy feeling in my head. After all these treatments, however, the condition did not improve. I tried all kinds of drugs likely to be effective, but in vain. At that time, I myself was studying and manufacturing vitamin preparations and fatigue-decreasing drugs. Frankly, I feel deeply disgusted to realize what useless things I was making.

For the cause of my illness, I needed only to look at my research assistants, who, like myself, were developing red sores on their noses and losing skin at the very time they were trying to develop medicines to improve the skin. I was poisoned with organic mercury.

To make matters worse, I was abusing my diet as well. Afterwards, reflecting upon the past, I noticed that the diet I took in this period of three-hours-a-day sleep consisted of either a hamburger steak or curry and rice. Every day I took curry and rice at lunch and hamburger steak at night either in my laboratory or in a bar, sipping a liquor along with it. This way of life lasted for more than ten years. Naturally my teeth went foul and my mental and physical strength fell.

Looking for the reasons for doing such an absurd thing I remembered an article about Ichizo Kobayashi, one of the greatest Japanese businessmen. It said that his secretary found him to be easy to satisfy as far as meals were concerned because all he wanted was a serving of hamburger steak and curry and rice.

Certainly, I held Mr. Kobayashi in high regard for his great success in business, but it was not for that reason that I stuck to the same dishes he did. The fact is, I was too busy to have time to prepare better meals. In spite of the fact that I was devoted to the idea of contributing to the health of mankind, I had no time to consider the balance of nutrition seriously. This was indeed like the physician who breaks his own rules of health.

This realization brought me to the great turning point of my life. As I will relate in more detail later, I rescued myself just in time from my chemical pursuits and turned my failing energy to the study of Chinese herb drugs. Like the diet of vegetables, potatoes, soybeans, millet grain and sardines which had saved me as a child, this new endeavor eventually led me to renewed vigor and success.

But I cannot say that I got away unpunished for my errors. In 1964, I lost Yamashiro. As a result of my failing health, I had to bring in new managers. They got control of my company and drove it into bankruptcy. Just as I stepped onto the threshold of developing a product that would really help mankind, I was forced to sell out to a giant company called Kanebo Industries. I became an employee of the firm and turned over to it all my inventions and patents.

The Vision of Hippocrates

I cannot help seeing a comparison between the story of my own health and the story of us all living in the modern world. We seek health today in everything from synthetic pharmaceuticals such as vitamin tablets to mercury-laden drugs. This practice is bringing us all to ruin. A good antidote for this erroneous perspective can be found in the saying of Hippocrates, the ancient Greek physician known as the father of medicine: "A disease is to be cured naturally by man's own power, and physicians help it."

In another civilization, another great man of medicine made the same discovery. It was Shin-huang-ti who, in the Ch'in era of China, compiled the fundamentals of Chinese medicine. He said: "It is diet which maintains true health and becomes the best drug."

These words I believe are true. And even though they were spoken thousands of years ago, long before the age of modern science, I believe we can still profit by them today.

This testimony from the past is not meant as an indictment of the accomplishments of the medical sciences to which the world owes much for the longer life expectancy and relief from disabling diseases enjoyed in the twentieth century. What I am suggesting is that these "medical" tools have had the unfortunate effect of corrupting attitudes toward health. This has gone so far, I fear, that now many people believe in medical and technological guarantees of good health, while little by little they give up their personal responsibility for the good health of their bodies.

In my own case, it was not until I turned to the words of Hippocrates and Shin-huang-ti with deep conviction that I began to recover from illness. In addition to this change in attitude, I credit my current state of excellent health to a regimen of Chinese herb drugs and a complete transformation of my diet which I at last adopted in desperation. Seeing the success this had, I dedicated the next ten years of my life to the pursuit of health in the pure, natural products of God's own Earth. As I will explain in the pages to come, my efforts focused on the juices of the green leaves of plants, and finally led to the discovery of the epochal health-promoting food extracted from the young leaves of barley.

At first this may strike you as a strange kind of food. But if you read on, I will explain how it can benefit your health and why this unusual form of food is so well adapted to the modern world.

To explain why I believe the modern world is in such great need of a new food, I must begin with a rather unpleasant task, that of tracing, in my own analysis, the path we have followed into an epoch of degraded health.

THE DEGRADATION OF MODERN-DAY HEALTH

It is well known, but still horrible for us to observe, that difficult-to-cure diseases including cancer, hypertension, cardiovascular diseases, liver diseases, renal diseases and neurosis are on the rise in spite of the best efforts of medical science. The underlying cause of these diseases, it seems to me, is not the failure of medical science, but the drastic changes we have brought upon our own physical constitution through the pollution of our environment, the deterioration of our nutrition and the misguided efforts of science to cure those faults with artificial solutions.

Even more widespread is the condition of degraded health as reflected in obesity, shoulder stiffness, lumbago, insomnia, constipation, allergy, aging skin, etc. Our unhealthy symptoms are indeed too many to count, and we may well say that those of us who are fortunate not to be diseased are at best only half-healthy.

To illustrate this point, statistics compiled in 1974 by the Japanese Ministry of Education showed that as many as 90 percent of children in primary schools had decayed teeth. In the age of the best dental care ever available to man, why should 90 percent of our children suffer from tooth decay?

When I was devoted to the study of pharmaceuticals, my mentor, Dr. Atsushi Fujita, warned me: "This is an era of Modern Medicine Almighty and of a belief in synthetic pharmaceuticals. But if such an era continues, mankind will suffer progressively from serious disease ten to twenty years from now."

At that time Japan relied on the introduction of new techniques from other countries. It imported sulfonamide drugs developed in Germany and penicillin and streptomycin developed in Britain. These antibiotics and other synthetic pharmaceuticals showed surprising effects against tuberculosis and other bacteria-induced diseases.

However, about 1965, there began an increase in the number of incurable and unusual diseases of which we had known little before, and also of various derangements in constitution. Now we are trying to find the right drugs to cure these diseases. But why? They cannot be cured by "synthetic solutions" because to a large extent they are the result of the "synthetic" products that are taking an ever larger place in our lives.

TOXINS IN THE ENVIRONMENT

Air, water and food are most important and essential to sustain our lives. There is no need to say much about the present condition of air, the first element for survival. Positive measures should be taken right away against industrial waste and motor vehicle exhaust. No living body which breathes air containing large quantities of nitrogen compounds, sulfur compounds and carbon monoxide can survive in good health. These pollutants enter the body and invade the cells where they combine with certain kinds of enzymes and DNA (nucleic acid) to disrupt normal life functions at a deep level of cellular activity usually unrecognized by most people.

We tend to take our water for granted. That is a serious mistake. Water not only quells thirst but also is an important means to supply essential minerals to our bodies. Degrading our supply of water will degrade our health.

Take the example of Lake Biwa, the largest lake in Japan and a source of municipal water. Large quantities of industrial waste, detergents, agricultural chemicals and chemical fertilizers dissolve in stream water that flows into Lake Biwa, polluting the water and causing excessive growth of algae. Since algae consume minerals, the water of Lake Biwa has been almost completely softened. Drinking water should be moderately hard, containing minerals such as calcium, magnesium and earth metals. Nowadays, people near Lake Biwa are forced to drink soft water all the time.

When we discuss the importance of water, we must reflect upon Kaschin-Beck disease, a degenerative bone disorder thought to be caused by the unhealthy water in the Tama River, the source of drinking water for the Tokyo metropolitan area. The true cause of Kaschin-Beck disease is not yet known, and active investigations are being conducted by a special project team of the Ministry of Welfare and Health. Some persons postulate that it is due to increased amounts of organic substances in the Tama River. I, however, suspect phosphate compounds used in detergents or synthetic additives. Soft water, lacking calcium and other minerals, is probably an accomplice. The combination of soft water and phosphates wreaks a terrible effect on the bones.

My suspicion follows experiments I once performed with a pharmacologist at a municipal sanitation test laboratory for a report entitled "The Effects of Foods on the Bones of Mice." The experiments involved sustaining mice with feed containing calcium and phosphoric acid in varying ratios. When the amount of phosphoric acid was increased beyond a certain limit, bone malformation occurred in the mice. Further increase of phosphoric acid in the food of pregnant mice yielded 40 malformed fetuses out of 100. I think the meaning of these results is self-evident.

Nor am I alone in this conclusion. A government warning was once issued to the manufacturer of a certain world-famous refreshing soft drink for its suspected effect on the bones of children because of the large amount of phosphoric acid contained in it.

From an overall consideration of these facts, I should say that my suspicion about the cause of Kaschin-Beck disease is not far from the truth.

The human body possesses vitality that can resist pollutants to some extent. But when the intrusions exceed a certain limit, our health rapidly suffers. The path of wisdom for us would be to remove the pollutants while our bodies still retain resisting power, and to take measures to strengthen that resisting power.

However, until people are able to accomplish these things, toxic substances will continue to pollute the atmosphere, the soil, the water, and even the food we eat.

Artificial Substances in Our Diet

At the same time as our environment is becoming more polluted by artificial substances, we are also subjecting our bodies to ever-greater stress through the substitution of synthetic products for the natural foods that once made up the entire diet of mankind.

I hesitate to try to list these fully. I could mention that we drink chemically-sweetened liquids; we eat foods artificially enhanced with vitamins and minerals; we consume substitutes for whipped cream that are 100 percent artificial; we even take chemicals to sleep and stay awake.

To demonstrate the pervasive and dangerous extent to which artificial substances have come to dominate our lives, I will offer one example which may seem insignificant enough until I show the damage it can cause.

Table salt seems harmless enough. But did you know it is commonly made by an artificial process? I believe this fact is linked to our loss of health. The table salt we now use is made by ion exchange membrane methods. It is sodium chloride with a purity of 99.9 percent which can be said to be a reagent-grade chemical, with a quality of tastelessness that you would expect to go along with that description. The good taste of natural salt comes from bittern, which contains minerals such as potassium, calcium and magnesium.

Officials at the Ministry of Welfare and Health and other concerned government organizations in Japan insist that minerals contained in natural salt are so slight they can be ignored. Certainly, the content of bittern in natural salt is only about 5 percent. However, Japanese pickle makers don't believe this 5 percent is insignificant. Japanese vegetable pickles, a product of fermentation, can only be made with natural salt because fermenting bacteria can only grow well with minerals as a nutrient source. The use of the present table salt, containing few minerals, cannot support tasty pickles.

If this were merely a problem of taste, there would not be much to worry about. But there are serious adverse effects caused by high-purity sodium chloride, now served as table salt. They are little known to the general public.

In 1972 when the production of table salt by evaporation of sea brine was superseded by the ion exchange resin membrane methods, the Council of Investigations of Table Salt, a non-governmental organization, conducted experiments on shellfish and goldfish to evaluate this new product. The results were not encouraging.

According to the experiments, the shellfish opened their shells and moved actively about when put in water containing natural salt dissolved in it. But they did so only slightly when put into water containing sodium chloride made by the ion exchange resin membrane method. Furthermore, it was reported that in natural salt water, ten goldfish survived for five days, whereas in sodium chloride water, eight out of ten goldfish died in two days.

This, I believe, was due to an imbalance of minerals within the cells of the experimental subjects caused by the reduced contents of minerals (e.g., potassium, calcium, magnesium) in water. The balance of minerals exerts very great effects on the living body, as I shall explain later.

The mineral deficiency in the table salt we now use should be regarded as a serious problem, since salt is essential to our daily life, and we are taking a fairly large amount of salt in all the foods we eat.

I once talked about this with an official at the salt division of the Japanese Monopoly Corporation. He, however, contended that the deficiency of minerals could be made up for by other foods.

But from what other foods? We can hardly receive adequate minerals from the meats, polished rice, refined bread and butter, refined sugar that make up the bulk of our diets. Neither can we benefit from the processed and preserved foods that make up the bulk of what can be found on the shelf of the modern super-market.

The modern economic system of mass production and mass selling has exposed us to great dangers. Heaps of food products are sold in supermarkets. The manufactur-ers are relying on huge-scale manufacturing facilities and masses of their products are transported over long distances. This naturally leads to the need for preserv-ing food products.

This need has stimulated the production of preserved foods using large amounts of salt and sugar, and also antiseptics. Many food stabilizers such as polyphosphates and artificial coloring agents have come into use. Furthermore, in order to disguise otherwise unfresh foods, the food industry is using all chemicals available. Their names—EDB, BHA, BHT, etc.—are becoming familiar to us through their constant repetition in newpapers. Some of these synthetic food additives have exerted drastic effects on the health of mankind.

DEPLETION OF NUTRIENTS IN THE NATURAL FOOD SUPPLY

The danger of antiseptics and food stabilizers may be somewhat ameliorated by the increasing use of freezing as a means of preserving food products. However, I do not, as some may, look upon the frozen food boom as a source of hope for the better nutrition of mankind. I will tell a story that illustrates my concern that frozen foods may actually be detrimental to good nutrition.

In Ireland one bleak winter, a spell of extremely cold weather was followed by a strange rash of paralysis in the limbs of sheep. Investigating the causes of the disease over the next several years, the British National

Institute of Nutrition turned up evidence that implicated the frostbitten grasses upon which the sheep were feeding. An important mineral called molybdenum, when consumed in these grasses, could be absorbed into the sheep's bloodstreams at only one-tenth the normal rate. The frost, it was learned, converted molybdenum in the frozen grasses into a form extremely difficult to absorb. Molybdenum, even in trace amounts, is essential to the body. Its deficiency caused malfunction of a specified enzyme which, in turn, induced leg paralysis.

I will examine the causes of that phenomenon. In raw vegetables and meats, minerals are bonded in an organic form to enzymes, proteins, amino acids and sugars inside individual cells. Scientifically, these are called organically bonded minerals. But upon heating or freezing, silicic acid, phosphoric acid and other compounds intrude upon those mineral bonds, converting the minerals into an inorganic state which is not easily absorbed by man and animals. It is as if the mineral were, in fact, removed from the food supply.

Exactly the same process occurs when fresh farm produce is frozen in commercial plants to afford it long-term shelf life. Its mineral content is locked into a form that becomes inaccessible to the human system. The food may fill the stomach and satisfy the taste buds, but it will not nurture the body to a healthy state.

Yet we are unable to do away with the current system of mass selling and resume the old system. Whether the present system is good or bad, we cannot turn back the clock. What can we do? We could look for a food made entirely of natural ingredients, all of the highest nutritional content, that can be mass-produced without cooking or freezing, stocked on the supermarket shelves and consumed as easily as the fast foods we have become accustomed to today. That, as I shall detail soon, is exactly what I have done. The salvation of our nutrition, I believe, will come not from cows on the hoof, not from fish or fowl, but from the green leaves of raw vegetables.

Color and Taste of Vegetables Tell of Depleted Quality

Green vegetables are not all alike. Some are inherently better for us than others, and many which are sold in the supermarkets today are next to worthless because of the agricultural mass-production techniques used to grow them and the depletion of the soils on which they were grown. Still others may also be contaminated with pesticide and herbicide toxins building up in the soil as a result of present-day farming practices which have already desecrated millions of acres of once valuable farmland in the United States.

Not only is the soil being polluted by agricultural chemicals, but it is gradually losing its inherent energy through chemical leaching. Falling to the earth in raindrops, nitrogen compounds, released into the air by industrial manufacturers, change to nitric acid and sulfuric acid. They penetrate into the earth and progressively dissolve alkaline metals contained in the soil, robbing it of minerals such as potassium and magnesium, which are the very source of the vitality of young green leaves, and also essential to the vitality of all forms of life. As this well-known "acid rain" is killing our rivers and lakes, chemical leaching is killing our farmland. Soil without minerals is dead soil and will cause serious defects in what we eat.

More and more of the vegetables and fruits we buy are grown in such soil and consequently are deficient in minerals. A variety of vegetables and fruits are now available throughout the year. We can eat tomato or cucumber even in the midst of winter. This is very convenient, and a luxury. But these vegetables are usually lighter in color, and the inherent taste of each vegetable is very much reduced. As a matter of fact, the taste and color of a vegetable are barometers of its mineral contents. The red or yellow of tomato or carrot and the green of lettuce or spinach become deeper as they contain more minerals. Vegetables sold in groceries, however, are light in color and do not taste good. This is because minerals within the soil are deficient, and the vegetables are forced in plastic greenhouses. The forced vegetables are well-shaped and big, but have extremely reduced mineral and vitamin contents. Such vegetables can be likened to the person who has gained weight from carbohydrates and fats.

Our sense of taste is subtle. Some persons accustomed to eating forced vegetables say that they dislike tomatoes grown in the right season under the direct sunlight because they taste unripe. But if they habitually ate the naturally-grown tomatoes, they would surely find them more tasty. In fact, farmers grow vegetables outdoors under the direct sunlight for their own consumption. The lesson is to not be fooled by a false sense of taste. We are born with good taste, but it can be perverted by wrong eating habits such as the common addiction to sugar and salt.

Certainly we cannot afford to reject those few high quality foods still available to us in this age of artificial foods and drugs, pollutants, toxic additives and depleted soil. Unfortunately, many people dislike vegetables and rely only on acidic foodstuffs. What will be their fate? In my opinion, they will be the half-diseased I mentioned earlier. Or the penalty could be exacted in a more subtle form.

The Damaging Effects of Undernourishment

A deficiency of green vegetables in the diet could be the cause of some of the cruelty in the public demeanor which often shocks us today. Once, while conducting an experiment with mice, I saw exactly such a thing happen. During the experiment, I noticed that mice fed for some time on a diet high in meat, but without grain or vegetables, gradually became cruel and finally they bit our hands when we tried to catch them in the cage. In contrast, mice fed vegetables and no meat were tame, showing no sign of biting. I was surprised to find that such a difference was caused within the same species by the difference in feed, although I had been well aware of the basic differences in nature between carnivorous and herbivorous animals.

I remember this experiment whenever a homicide is reported in newspapers and on television. Frequently, manslaughter occurs inexplicably among relatives and neighbors, attributable only to sheer madness. I suspect with horror that an unbalanced diet, as in the case of mice fed only meat, could be an accomplice to the crime.

Americans are now familiar with this phenomenon because of the bizarre case of Dan White, who inexplicably murdered two of his colleagues on the San Francisco Board of Supervisors. In court, White presented the defense that he was temporarily insane from eating cupcakes at the time of the shooting. As a matter of criminal justice, we may find the explanation inadequate, but I believe it has a basis in fact. Today, studies have become commonplace showing that abnormal emotional behavior in some children can be corrected by reducing acidic foods in the diet.

The mind can pursue this connection to a disturbing

extreme. How can we know that an otherwise "sane" person with his hand on the launch button of a nuclear warhead may not be deprived of his sanity in the same way as the mice, and turn his hand against the family of man, bringing us all to ruin? It is an unpleasant thought I raise in the hope that a measure of prevention will always be exercised.

In a quite different way, the encroachment of artificial foods into our diet will, I fear, push us into an equally dangerous drift by distorting and malforming the human design genetically. The ill effects of chemicals and artificial food additives on genes are widely acknowledged and are being studied throughout the world. I will comment only to the extent of describing how these ill effects might work in degenerating the genetic chain, called deoxyribonucleic acid (DNA). In DNA, four kinds of special bases are bonded in a special manner along with a protein consisting of about twenty types of amino acids. The action of the protein decides which genes are to be active and which are not. It is said that of the 10,000 types of genes, about 3,000 are in actual operation. Many of the remaining genes are considered useless at present, having served their purpose earlier in the course of man's evolution.

What would happen if these genes should begin to act randomly? It does happen, in fact, when foreign matter taken into the body finds its way to the proteins which govern the activities of the genes and forms a bond. The damaged protein is no longer able to control the genes. This naturally leads to the abnormal cell divison we call cancer, and malformation.

Cancer, malformation, cruelty, malaise—in view of these dangers I have described, I am not surprised to observe the growth of movements seeking to take us "Back to Nature," in the way we feed ourselves as well as treat the ailments of the body. I believe that the world is now slowly moving in that direction. But we, living in the present age, cannot wait for such a change. At the very least, we should each begin a revolution of our own, a revolution to cleanse our bodies of chemicals and foreign substances. This can be done right away if we so decide.

CHAPTER 2

THE GREEN REVOLUTION
VS. CHEMICALS AND DRUGS

NATURE PROVIDES THE KEY TO GOOD HEALTH

NOW IS THE TIME when we should stop to reflect upon the marvelous vitality of the earth, which expresses itself most profoundly in the cycle of the green leaf.

Each spring, those trees and plants which have retained their vitality even in the dormant state sprout small buds which soon grow into green leaves. The leaves become darker in color and grow as a result of receiving energy from the sun, dews from heaven and nutrients from the earth.

When spring comes, we feel relieved to see the mountains and fields again covered with green. Like the leaves, we are refreshened and regain our vigor. This the philosophers know. But is the power of green so small as to be restricted only to the psyche of man? Would we say it is negligible in its effect on the physical world of man? I cannot but feel that man has overlooked the power of green in favor of science and technology and modern rationalism.

Were it not for an abundance of green in this world, no animals, not to mention human beings, could survive.

Even in the African and Middle Eastern deserts, plants and green grasses and trees sprouting in oases sustain the chain of animal life. Places without green grasses and trees may well be said to be the dead world. Indeed, it is no exaggeration to say that since the beginning of life on earth, no animal has been able to live without green.

Chlorophyll Is Similar in Chemical Structure to Human Blood

As the green leaf is a symbol of the vitality of the earth, red blood is the symbol of the vitality of higher animal life. I postulate that there is a structural, as well as symbolic, similarity between the green leaves of the earth and the red blood in our veins.

We breathe oxygen in the air and discharge carbon dioxide gas. The leaves of a plant, in the process of a reaction called "photosynthesis," breathe carbon dioxide gas and discharge oxygen. Without oxygen, of course, we could not survive.

I have heard that the quantity of oxygen required by man and other animals throughout Japan far exceeds that supplied by our country's green vegetation. This is partly because Japan's population, which was about 30 million in 1875, has now increased to about 120 million, and partly because the amount of oxygen used by industrial establishments has increased enormously. The deficiency, we are told, is continuously made up for by oxygen carried on transcontinental air currents all the way from the Amazon region of South America. Thus, it is as though we Japanese were importing oxygen created by the Amazon jungle. How ironic it is that Japan, which has to import most raw materials from abroad, must now import even this vital source of life for her people. Yet we know that we are all, like Japan, importing the source of our lives in the food we eat.

Natural "Green" Neglected at the Dinner Table

Health means that the management of life activities within the body is normal. To maintain health, we must provide our bodies a balanced supply of minerals such as potassium, magnesium and calcium. Of these, potassium is of utmost importance, for it is contained inherently in the cells of all living organisms as a source of life activity. But within the bodies of men living in the present day, potassium and other minerals are found in much reduced quantities. This does not need to be the case, because nature provides us a healthy supply of all minerals. All we need to do is look for them in the right place. But we cannot expect them to float to us on the transcontinental air currents as oxygen floats to Japan.

The greening of our national lands is a much-applauded goal today and its importance has gained widespread recognition. The Green Revolution initiated by young American scientists was based on an understanding of the power of green foods. The trend is a good one. But as things stand, something essential is still lacking. Just look around at our dinner tables. How much green is there? Take a look at the food-selling sites of department stores and supermarkets. How much raw vegetable is there? Maybe less than 1 percent of the entire floor space for foods. The remainder is for artificially colored candies, acidic foods such as meat and fish, and processed food products such as canned foods, sausages and refrigerated food products, and so on. Most of us are vaguely aware that green foods are important to maintain health. But today when commercialism has priority in commodity distribution, raw vegetables can occupy only a small percentage of the entire sales site in markets, and convenient processed foods are overwhelming them. The status of vegetables in our diet has therefore been debased.

We cannot but say that this is the very reason our health has been impaired. Raw green cannot be replenished by other greens. I think that it is now the time when we need a cleansing revolution of our blood—by increasing our intake of green vegetables—along with the greening revolution of the national land.

In this chapter, I will describe the work I have conducted over the past twenty years to help make this possible.

ANALYSIS OF NATURE'S BEST RAW MATERIALS

Having been inspired by the sayings of Hippocrates and Shin-huang-ti, I began a personal search for a food which would promote good health by vitalizing the body's own power of healing. I restudied Chinese herb drugs and also investigated the nutrients in many foods which have been known for their healing properties from ancient times.

After conducting extensive investigation, I settled upon the use of "green juices" of vegetables as the richest source of nutrient available to man. Green vegetable juices contain high concentrations of the minerals, enzymes and vitamins which are essential to good health and to the discharge of pollutants attacking the body.

That conclusion, I believe, is fairly widely accepted. But the next step in my research, leading to my focus on the leaves of green barley, required a little inspiration, some unexpected advice from my former teacher and, finally, a lot of dabbling in the kitchen which I have to admit did not always earn a four-star rating.

Quite by accident, my inspiration came to me on a farm. When I began to work on green vegetable juices, I happened to visit a dairy farmer in the Chita Peninsula in the southwestern part of Japan. I remember it was summer, but I could see no rice paddies which normally grow at this time of the year in every part of Japan. Instead, I saw Italian ryegrass, rye and oats growing in thick green over a large tract of land. At that time, the harvest of rice could sell at about $1,600 per acre, while the leaves of rye per acre yielded only about $120. I naturally questioned the farmer as to why he squandered his fields on a less valuable crop. His answer was that when he fed his cows the leaves of rye, they yielded more milk, amounting to an annual increase of about $4,900, than when he fed them withered grasses or imported pasture grasses. The farmer added that the milkable period of cows fed rye would be prolonged by five or six years.

I was astonished to learn of the ability of green leaves to create so much vitality and energy.

Moved by this experience, I collected and analyzed leaves from every vegetable or grass available, if they were green at all. Then, discarding the many plants that were obviously not suitable, I narrowed them down to about 150 kinds of green-leaved plants. Each one of these I prepared in a juice which I drank myself and also tried on my relatives. That test was enough to eliminate many. In fact, it proved easy to eliminate even many of the green plants which hold high reputations as nutrient sources.

The Disadvantages of Spinach, Chlorella and Other Well-Known Foods

Since I was seeking the deepest green leaves, I eliminated lettuce, Chinese cabbage, cabbage, and celery quickly as unsuitable because of their light tone of green. Green pepper, persimmon leaves and pine needles do contain effective ingredients, but on the other hand they were too pungent for use as green juices in the daily diet. Spinach has soft green leaves and high alkalinity, and seems to be a superior raw material for green juice. However, it has a low mineral content and contains calcium in the form of calcium oxalate which is hard to assimilate and may cause bone softening if taken in excess. Furthermore, it is believed that calcium oxalate build-up within the body may induce nephrolithiasis and cystolithiasis.

In addition to the species cited above, I collected the leaves of loquat, mango, strawberry, mulberry, parsley and radish. However, I excluded drug herbs such as aloe, cranesbill, *Houttuynia cordata*, knotweed and *Swertia japonica*. Although they are drugs, they also contain poisonous components and are unsuitable for daily diet.

I made powders of various green juices from the plant leaves collected. During the course of my experiments, I found that the leaves of plants growing actively in the summertime had a number of bacteria and fungi adhering to them. In particular, I found that the leaves of comfrey, radish and parsley permitted easy adhesion of bacteria and fungi because of numerous hairs, creases and depressions on their surfaces. The bacteria and fungi were found to be difficult to remove even by washing.

I gave special attention to chlorella, which is often considered a beneficial food. But I did not find it so. Plants and microorganisms such as chlorella which man and other animals have avoided from old are likely to contain components which are unsuitable for them. Chlorella is an algae which has a deep green color. For over seven years I studied the properties, toxicity and edibility of chlorella. The cell membrane of chlorella, as a single-celled plant, is made of a chitinous substance which is as hard as a fingernail. In an attempt to produce a green juice from chlorella, I treated it in various ways so as to destroy this hard cell membrane physically or chemically, but failed completely. Chlorella has been much studied in Germany for more than forty years as a possible source of protein. German workers found that because of the hard cell membrane, chlorella is hard to digest, and, what is worse, it possesses genes which have shown no appreciable evolution for more than 3,000 million years since the plant first appeared on earth. Because of these unhealthy factors, chlorella has not gained acceptance in Germany and other European countries.

Recently, newspapers reported that according to Tokyo Hygiene Testing Laboratory, many people suffer from eczema and skin inflammation after taking chlorella.

More evidence came in against chlorella some time ago when a leading Japanese foodstuffs company purchased a chlorella manufacturing company and produced chlorella-containing yogurt and lactobacillus drinks by incorporating an extract of chlorella in a nutrient culture medium for lactobacilli. The company launched a nationwide sales campaign. Later, the research staff of this company became aware that the extract of chlorella contained components which are hazardous to the human body. At enormous loss, the company stopped selling these chlorella-containing drinks. They also removed many display panels bearing the phrase "Chlorella-Containing Drink" which had been erected throughout the nation. The measure was a courageous one.

Moving on in my search, I found the leaves of bamboo grass and rice plants to have large quantities of extremely hard fibrous tissues. Because of this, a green juice could scarcely be extracted from the bamboo leaves.

Finally, chickweeds, asters, pigweeds, clovers, kudzu,

acacias, Japanese ivies and peas stood the test, and proved to have merit as raw material for green juices. It was found, however, that these plants fell short in regard to the contents of active ingredients such as minerals, vitamins, enzymes and chlorophyll.

Of all the plants I tested, the young leaves of barley and certain other cereal grasses proved throughout my testing to have the most remarkable quantities of active ingredients. Figure 1 shows a sampling of these results.

FIGURE 1
Breakdown by Percent of the Major Components of Green Barley Essence, as Compared to Other Vegetable Powders

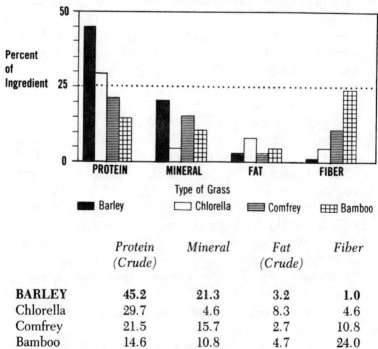

	Protein (Crude)	Mineral	Fat (Crude)	Fiber
BARLEY	**45.2**	**21.3**	**3.2**	**1.0**
Chlorella	29.7	4.6	8.3	4.6
Comfrey	21.5	15.7	2.7	10.8
Bamboo	14.6	10.8	4.7	24.0

A Staple for Thousands of Years

Young barley leaves, I discovered, were relatively free from each of the specific faults I found in other plants.

Among the plants I studied, only barley sprouts rapidly grow to young leaves in temperatures below 15°C, when even fungi and bacteria cannot grow. Naturally, therefore, the young leaves of barley are cleaner than vegetables grown in the summertime. In addition, as the leaves are smooth on the surface, any foreign matter on them can be readily washed away. Early harvest has another benefit in reducing the likelihood of insect infestation, thus making organic growing of the plant feasible.

Our taste, as I have mentioned, is a tool which can be perverted. Yet, it is a vital tool which incorporates the wisdom of the centuries. If followed wisely, it can distinguish for us those foods which have proved successful for man.

The foods we eat should be required to be essentially free from harshness, strong odors and pungent components. For example, strong odor is indicative of a high content of perfumery components. These components have more or less germicidal effects. The flavors of condiments consist solely of volatile components, most of which are aldehydes and ester oils. Summer vegetables and plants growing in the hot southern countries have strong aromatic odors. This is because these aromatic components of the plants have their own power of preventing decay and insect infestation. The extremely strong aromatic odors of mangoes, bananas and pineapples are also examples.

These germicidal components are unnecessary for our healthy bodies. Rather they are very likely to act as toxic components which impart some stimulus to our living cells. It is true, however, that they could awaken our inactivated organs by giving a slight stimulus. For example, when secretion of the gastric juice has gone wrong, it can be promoted by a certain amount of spice in the diet. I admit this efficacy, but still insist that spicy foods should not be taken habitually in large quantities.

It must be due to the absence of any pungent or other displeasing taste that barley, rice and other cereals have been selected as main staples in the daily diet. This is the wisdom of mankind, and I believe that it is more scientific than modern science.

Thus, I concluded that among the variety of green vegetables available to man, cereal grasses stood at the top of the list. They are highest in the active ingredients that are vital to the proper nutrition of the living body; they are free of germicidal and fungal contamination; and they have been selected by mankind for centuries as staple foods.

I must clearly delineate here that I am speaking of the leaves of these cereal grasses, rather than their kernels, which, I must admit, have clearly been the preference of man in his historical eating habits.

I strongly suspect that the reason man has not favored the grasses of cereals is because of the high content of cellulose fiber which forms the structure of these tall grasses. Leaf-eating animals are supplied with a set of teeth especially designed for grinding these cellulose fibers to release the nutrients within. The human tooth arrangement can handle all vegetables, but is not really equipped to break down large quantities of leafy material. However, a comparison of the contents of the leaves of barley against the grain of other plants, as shown in Table 5, demonstrates that there would be a clear nutritional advantage to the grass.

TABLE 5
Comparison of Ingredients of Green Barley Essence, Polished Rice and Wheat Germ Harvested per 10 Ares (0.247 Acres)

Nutrient	Green Barley Essence (160 kg)	Wheat Grain (314 kg)	Ratio: Barley to wheat	Polished Rice (340 kg)	Ratio: Barley to rice
Proteins	72.30 kg	31.71 kg	2.27	21.08 kg	3.46
Fats	5.07	5.96	0.85	2.72	1.87
Carbohydrates	37.00	232.00	0.16	240.00	0.15
Potassium	14,200.0 g	1,133.0 g	12.90	384.0 g	36.50
Calcium	1,184.0	94.0	12.80	20.0	59.00
Vitamin B_1	2.06	0.94	2.19	0.3	6.80
Vitamin C	211.4	0.0	Infinite	0.0	Infinite
Vitamin E	81.6	8.1	10.00	1.36	60.00

Notice that the barley leaves contain proteins in an amount more than three times that of polished rice and more than two times that of wheat grain. In addition, the barley leaf proves to be significantly richer in vitamins and minerals.

The caloric value of the barley leaves, on the other hand, is less than that of rice or wheat grain. But when considering the amount of the barley leaves that can be harvested each year, their caloric value is more than double those of rice or wheat grains. Rice grains or wheat or barley grains can be harvested once a year—twice at most. But the leaves of barley can be harvested throughout the year if only we sow the seed, and where climate permits we can expect up to five rotations a year. If calculated on this basis, the protein content of the barley leaves that can be harvested would amount to more than ten times the protein yield of rice or barley grass harvested on the same area of land.

It was clear to me, then, that the leaves of the cereal grasses provide the nearest thing this planet offers to the perfect food. For reasons of palatability, higher nutrient content and favorable harvesting features, green barley stands out as the best among these. The only defect I would say I could find, as far as its applicability to man, was its high content of cellulose fiber which made chewing difficult. All that was lacking, then, was a method to extract those nutrients from the plant and make it available to the consumer in an easy-to-use form.

With this conclusion as my starting point, I set out to develop the potential of green barley leaves as the ideal food for man. The result of my effort was Green Barley Essence.

CHAPTER 3

THE ESSENCE OF GREEN BARLEY

CRITERIA FOR THE IDEAL FAST FOOD

THERE IS an old saying in Japan, and I believe the sentiment is shared by all who are aware of nutrition, to the effect that food should be eaten raw to give the most benefit to the human body. Green Barley Essence is none other than the pure, raw, uncooked essence of one of nature's best foods.

Inherently, I believe, the human body is created to sustain itself on raw foods. Our primitive ancestors ate only raw foods, but learned to soften harder foods with the heat of a fire. Gradually, cooking came to serve the purpose of purification and disease control. The practice of cooking everything should be seriously questioned now that other processes can serve that purpose.

I am sure that old Japanese expression was first uttered long before mankind had any alternative to eating food in its natural state. It is only in the last century or two that we have begun mixing chemical processes with the production of food.

I think the word "natural" could be placed in that old saying without in the least offending the wise souls who first uttered it.

The Japanese, as you probably know, are famous for their habit of eating the flesh of fish raw. However, even in Japan, green barley leaves have not found a prominent place in the supermarket vegetable stands or on the dinner table any more than in America. But that is not really necessary, since the same benefits can be obtained by consuming the nutrients of barley in the concentrated and easy-to-use form I have provided. In fact, the benefits are actually greater, since Green Barley Essence provides the nutrients of green barley in a pure, easily-assimilated essence, much like a health food juice.

More Effective than Vegetables Eaten Raw

Those who are interested in health have long been aware that green juices obtained by crushing and squeezing vegetables are far more beneficial than ordinary vegetables eaten raw. Let us consider why this is true.

As vegetables contain fibrous tissues, we must eat them in considerable quantity if we are to receive the required amounts of their active ingredients. The green juice is an essence of active ingredients remaining after removal of fibrous tissues. By nature a much more concentrated form, even a small amount of vegetable juice contains abundant active ingredients. I do not intend to detract from the importance of fiber in the diet, the value of which is well documented. Rather, I am suggesting that the nutritional benefits of cereal grasses become most accessible after the fibers in the plant are removed.

Unfortunately, many people experience repugnance at the thought of drinking the juice of green vegetables, even though they find the vegetables quite palatable in the raw form. Strange as it may seem, this is evidence of one of the most important benefits of vegetable juices—that they are very readily digestible and absorbable. In raw leafy vegetables, the nutrients are enclosed inside the fibrous cell walls and so cannot be directly absorbed by the mucous membrane of the oral cavity. Juicing extracts the nutrients from within the cells, allowing the active ingredients to make direct contact with the mucous membrane and immediately act on the gustatory nerves there. This direct contact tends to make green juices strong-tasting.

Moreover, the stomach and intestinal tract of man lack sufficient quantities of cellulase, an enzyme which aids the digestion of bulky materials and is needed to fully assimilate raw vegetables. Green juices can be completely and easily assimilated, however. When a person drinks a green juice, its ingredients are taken into the cells, and promptly revive cells which have become distressed.

Because of the advantages of green juices, they have aroused considerable interest since the 1950s. But the campaigns encouraging their use were not always as successful as anticipated. The reason can generally be ascribed to taste. The old saying goes: "Good medicines taste bitter." But in practice, if the green juices taste harsh, they prove unsuitable for long-term use. Thus, green juices, above all, must meet the criteria of taste.

Common raw materials available for green juices include, for example, chickweeds, asters, pigweeds, clovers, kudzu, acacias, Japanese ivies, peas, lettuce, Chinese cabbage, cabbage, onion, celery, green pepper, persimmon leaves and pine needles. I have already discussed the nutritional disadvantages of some of these. On top of that, anyone who could drink these juices would be a masochist indeed. Something more pleasant is needed.

Happily, I discovered, the leaves of young barley, even when taken in the form of juice, remain exceptionally palatable, tasting something like a green tea with a fresh pea or light spinach flavor. That was one point in my favor when I started out, more than twenty years ago, to develop a food which would meet those demands I mentioned above. To reiterate, the requirements were for a pure, raw vegetable juice that would be pleasant to taste. To fit into the modern world, it had to be easy to purchase, easy to use, and stable over a long period of time. Let me add one more criterion, lest it be taken for granted. I also required that this new food should be completely natural.

It would have been simple enough to grow and harvest young barley leaves. But how could these be eaten raw? It doesn't really seem like an appealing idea. And, more important, how could they be delivered to the consumer in a form that would easily fit into the fast-paced life we have today? And how could this food be preserved and distributed in its completely natural form? All these questions added up to one conclusion. I was not merely looking for the ideal food. What I wanted was something with a modern look and form, an ideal "fast food." That idea was primary in my mind more than twenty years ago when I focused my efforts upon the leaves of the barley plant.

Even before I selected green barley leaves as the raw material for this new product, I had already made some progress on developing the method I would use to make this remarkable transformation.

Although I have described Green Barley Essence as a juice, it actually comes in solid form, either as a powder or tablet, both of which are stable to decomposition during storage and are thus free from the fatal defect of ordinary green juices, which will seldom last longer than a day, even if refrigerated. When dissolved in water, Green Barley Essence is substantially the same as the fresh green juice.

How is this accomplished?

Green Barley Essence is made by dehydrating a green juice of the young leaves of barley to a fine powder at room temperature within a time as short as 2 to 3 seconds, using a spray-drying process which has been patented in many countries of the world including Japan and the United States.

My interest in this process goes back to the turning point in my life when I finally embraced the wisdom of Hippocrates and turned to Chinese herb drugs to help restore my body to health.

PRODUCTION OF GREEN BARLEY ESSENCE

Chinese herb drugs, imported into Japan in ancient times, have never lost their appeal with the Japanese people and are used to this day as a treatment for many ailments. The interest in these ancient herbal cures remains so great, in fact, that many Japanese companies are involved in research developing new health products from these formulas.

My research in this field, which began around 1960, proved quite fruitful for me commercially. I succeeded in extracting a substance called Swertiamalin from *Swertia japonica*, used as a gastrointestinal drug. This became a primary ingredient in my hair preparation, which sold under the name Shiden. Then I isolated ephedrine from the herbal medicine called *Ma huang*, which comes from a small evergreen tree growing naturally in northern China and Mongolia. This proved successful as a remedy for asthma. In all, I developed about thirty products from Chinese herbs.

Traditionally, the leaves of Chinese herbs are steeped in hot water so the formula can be ingested as a heavy tea. The special knowledge required to prepare herbal medicines and the associated inconvenience and often bitter taste probably prevents many people from using these cures when they should.

In the course of my research, I decided to look for a way to make herbal tea as easy to use as instant coffee. Naturally, I thought of using the same process which brought the world instant coffee. I hired the Swenson Company, which manufactures ships and military tanks in the United States, to build a small spray-dry plant in Takatsuki. I boiled vats of herbal tea and spray-dried the liquid at the lowest possible temperature. This produced ancient Chinese medicines in a convenient powder form.

As I mentioned earlier, when my company was forced into bankruptcy in 1964, I went to work as an executive for the Kanebo Company, a giant Japanese drug manufacturer which bought out all my patents. My technique of spray drying had proved so successful with herb drugs that I began to think about the possibility of producing a high-quality food the same way.

To pursue this new idea on my own, I left Kanebo in 1967. With $40,000 which I borrowed from my sisters and brothers, I started a new company called Japan Natural Foods Company, Ltd. As I have already described, countless experiments and consultations with my former teacher, Dr. Fujita, led me to concentrate all my efforts on barley leaves.

The work did not go as smoothly as I had hoped it would. At first, I was told by people who used my product that it was not effective. I realized I was subjecting the barley to too much heat during the drying. Coffee is spray-dried at a temperature of 130° F so that it will be slightly scorched for aroma. However, that temperature is much too high for drying barley because it kills the active ingredients.

Once I worked out a method for drying the barley juice at a far lower temperature, I ran into more trouble when the product I sold turned brown in its container after several months. This problem almost forced me out of business in 1969. But I finally found the solution.

In the meantime, I had much to learn about the harvesting of barley. It is, of course, vital to allow as little time as possible to pass between cutting, washing, juicing and powdering the plant. I found that freshly harvested plants packed under canvas in a truckbed would begin to generate their own heat in a very few hours and turn brown. To prolong the storage time, I tried freezing the plants, but that too killed many of the active ingredients. Eventually, I learned that the only proper method was to locate the production facility near the barley fields.

Many demanding standards must be met in the farming itself. The barley must be grown free of pesticides and herbicides. Though this raises its cost, I insist upon it.

I have also found that there is a precise time to do the harvesting. The leaves of barley grow rapidly in the early spring, and become deep green as they absorb minerals and water from the earth and sunlight. Green is the very symbol of minerals in the earth; vitamin and protein contents also increase in proportion to the density of green.

The green of the young leaves of barley is especially thick and deep, and the young leaf can grow by 2 or 3 centimeters overnight. Green Barley Essence must be extracted from the leaves at this most vital stage.

An analysis of the barley leaf according to its stages of

growth shows why it is important to harvest at this early stage. As the chart below illustrates, young leaves with a height of about 20 cm in the early primordial stage contain the largest amounts of active ingredients. Leaves with a height of 45 to 60 cm yield progressively less active ingredients.

TABLE 6

Comparison of the Composition of Extracts of the Leaves of Barley at Different Heights

Nutrient	20 cm	45 cm	60 cm
Crude Protein	45.20 %	27.90 %	20.34 %
Digestible Protein	41.8	25.99	18.49
Potassium	5.99	4.42	4.41
Carbohydrates	23.20	48.25	57.77
(mg% equals 1,000th of 1 percent)			
Reduced Vitamin C	328.8 mg%	140.5 mg%	123.5 mg%
Vitamin E	1.45	1.35	1.31
Calcium	1,108.0	851.9	691.5

The patented process that I have described makes the essence of young green barley available without causing degeneration or decomposition of the effective components such as proteins, vitamins, enzymes, minerals and chlorophyll. The resulting product can be stored for long periods of time.

Natural Nutrition in a Concentrated Form

Dr. Tatsuji Kobori, head of Yokohama Teishin Hospital, has taken an interest in green juices for decades, but always complained of unpalatability. When I recently met him, I mixed some Green Barley Essence into a glass of water and let him taste it. Astonished, he agreed to its palatability, and said it would be acceptable even to those who have an aversion to "green juices." He encouraged me to publicize Green Barley Essence as a source of health rather than to make synthetic pharmaceuticals.

Mr. Yasusaburo Sugi, Professor Emeritus of Tokyo University of Education, once confided: "This powderized Green Barley Essence would be just what is suitable to those who appreciate the effectiveness of green juice for health but feel it troublesome to make it by themselves."

About 3g (about 1.5 teaspoonsful) of the powdery Green Barley Essence is the equivalent of 100g (two handfuls) of the young leaves of fresh barley. The nutrients contained in it equal 300g of cabbage or more than one head of lettuce. As shown in Table 7, a favorite health food such as wheat germ cannot compare to Green Barley Essence as a concentrated source of nutrients.

TABLE 7
Comparison of Ingredients of Green Barley Essence
and Wheat Germ (%)

	Green Barley Essence	*Wheat Germ*
Protein	45.2 %	27.9 %
Fiber	1.0	2.1
Minerals	21.3	4.1
Trace Ingredients: (mg% equals 1,000th of 1%)		
Vitamin B1	1.3mg%	2.1mg%
Vitamin B2	2.75	0.6
Nicotinic Acid	10.6	7.0

How to Use Green Barley Essence

I recommend taking it two or three times a day in a dosage of 1g for infants, and 2g to 6g for school children and adults. For those who have an acidic constitution or who have the symptoms of diseases that I will describe in later chapters, twice the ordinary dose is recommended. Before taking, put the powder in a beverage glass and add water to it to the desired concentration.

At first, the powder may not be as palatable to you as other foods. But it does not taste harsh, and on continued ingestion, people do find it tasty. At the right ratio of powder to water, the taste almost disappears, yielding only a pleasant, refreshing taste. Added to milk, it gives a malty taste and improves digestion of the milk. It is also exceptionally tasty with tomato or carrot juice or sprinkled on salads and even ice cream.

As an alternative, you may take it in tablet form with water. It will naturally become a green juice within the stomach. But it is more effective to dissolve it in water beforehand. Upon drinking it, a part of the Green Barley Essence is immediately absorbed from the mucous membrane of the oral cavity.

It is best to drink three glasses of Green Barley Essence every day. If taken on an empty stomach in the morning, Green Barley Essence brings life to the mind and blood as well as coffee does, at the same time providing a shot of nutrition for the day instead of acid and caffeine. It also helps drive off afternoon drowsiness. Take the third glass just before retiring to bed to lower acidity in the blood and aid sleep.

It should be noted that Green Barley Essence in powder form is unstable at high temperatures. When dissolved in water warmer than 120° F, the important enzymes, vitamins and chlorophyll will be lost. Therefore, take it dissolved in either cold water or water at room temperature. Furthermore, Green Barley Essence seems to be more effective when sipped, rather than gulped down.

I cannot definitely say how long Green Barley Essence should be taken to obtain relief from a specific symptom. In one case, a woman who suffered from gastritis and had been taking drugs and injections for some time without success felt better after only one glass of Green Barley Essence dissolved in water. In some persons the results seem to appear slowly. It is very rare, however, that no change is observed after more than three months' continued administration. Since the effect of Green Barley Essence appears at different times with different people, it is important to continue taking it patiently if one wants to use it for curative purposes.

Even when taken excessively, Green Barley Essence never affects the body adversely. It is like eating raw vegetables, which even in excessive quantities, cause no trouble to the body. The only difference is that Green Barley Essence has a higher content of a wider variety of active ingredients.

I must point out that some mild effects can be associated with the first use of Green Barley Essence. Since it is taken mostly as a solution in cold water, some persons may develop temporary diarrhea if they drink too much. In this case, the amount should be gradually increased, starting with ½ teaspoon in 4 ounces of water, to accustom the stomach and intestines. Conversely, others may develop constipation as a result of drinking too much. This is caused by the ease with which Green Barley Essence is digested, since it is free from fibrous tissues. The constipation can be quickly cured by eating other vegetables at the same time.

Persons with eczema or pimples may notice a temporary aggravation of their symptoms when they begin to drink Green Barley Essence. This is a phenomenon called "mengen" which is also experienced with Chinese herb drugs. If it occurs, reducing the beginning dosage will alleviate, and finally clear, the symptoms.

Hypervitaminosis, a condition caused by excess vitamin ingestion, has recently attracted attention. However, most cases of hypervitaminosis are associated with synthetic vitamin preparations in high dosages. Almost no problem occurs with natural vitamins. Since Green Barley Essence contains various vitamins in a well-balanced state, its use cannot result in an excessive intake of a particular type of vitamin.

Carotene, contained in a fairly high quantity in Green Barley Essence, is converted to vitamin A upon entering the body. It is said that ingestion of an excess of vitamin A can be harmful, but this refers to intake of pure vitamin A in high quantity. The carotene in Green Barley Essence is called provitamin A and it becomes vitamin A only after entering the body. It cannot cause hypervitaminosis.

Whenever a curative process is initiated in a body adapted to the condition of disease, a phenomenon called "the healing crisis" may occur, causing pain or discomfort as the body readjusts. If this should occur with the use of Green Barley Essence, large quantities of fresh water and a stoic approach are the best recourse.

CHAPTER 4

A STOREHOUSE OF ACTIVE INGREDIENTS

THE FIVE ESSENTIAL NUTRIENTS

IN THE previous chapter, I stated that Green Barley Essence contains surprisingly great amounts of active components such as minerals, enzymes, chlorophyll and vitamins. Adding proteins to that list, I would call these the five essential nutrients.

I think it is safe to say that the importance of these five nutrients—especially minerals, vitamins and proteins—in maintaining the health and vitality of the body is universally acknowledged. But I am not so certain whether the public is adequately informed on the strengths and weaknesses of various popular food products in supplying these vital nutrients. Or that even those who know which foods are best for them can resist the attraction of processed, artificially preserved, grease-filled foods characteristic of our modern culture. I seriously doubt it.

As I have already suggested, Green Barley Essence can be a kind of antidote for the deteriorated nutrition of the fast-food culture because it is a fast food that is totally natural and yet higher than any other natural food in the essential five ingredients.

44

In this chapter, I shall examine these five ingredients in detail. I will explain why they are important to health and present research statistics to document the superior content of each of these ingredients in Green Barley Essence compared to other popular foods.

To begin this discussion, I would like to acknowledge the contribution of my former teacher, Professor Atsushi Fujita, Chief of the Department of Pharmacy, Kumamoto University. It was Dr. Fujita who first analyzed the barley leaf chemically, extensively published research on its rich nutrient contents and placed this information in the context of a biological theory.

Dr. Fujita was one of the leading scholars of organic chemistry before World War II. He went into the field of pharmacology, dreaming of synthesizing life. Professor Fujita studied with Dr. Nagayoshi Nagai, a world-famous pharmacologist, and later worked at the Koch Institute in Germany.

Dr. Fujita once told me an interesting story about the nature of life. When studying at the Koch Institute, he said, he pondered for three days and three nights near the Rhine River, groping for a theory of life. Exhausted, he took a stroll and, while resting under the sun on the bank of the Rhine, he saw a large barley field spread below him. He had been there three days before and saw only small buds coming out. Yet, in the cold winter when no other plants had yet sprouted any buds, the barley was issuing vivid green young leaves. He was greatly inspired by the amazing vitality of barley.

This experience became an incentive to the formulation of the life theory Dr. Fujita sought. Called the theory of the Organic Concept Chart, it received world-wide attention at that time.

The gist of this theory is as follows: All living substances have two characters, an organic character and an inorganic character. A living organism, including the human being, possesses a balance of the organic and inorganic characters, and these are just about equal in percentage. Thus, in order to maintain a well-balanced body and promote health, the ideal food is a natural raw food composed of about half organic and half inorganic properties.

Many synthetic pharmaceuticals are either excessively inorganic or excessively organic. Diseased persons may benefit from them, if they are taken temporarily. But on long-term administration, they do not maintain balance within the living body but rather break it.

Dr. Fujita formed the conclusion that the young leaves of barley, the first plants to sprout after winter dormancy, are nurtured in soil that has stored minerals in high concentrations and would therefore be the most effective food for sustaining life. He based this conclusion on his belief that the source of life elements in all living organisms resides in minerals contained in the earth.

On one visit, Dr. Fujita told me:

"At the age of seventy-one now, after fifty years of devotion to pharmacological studies, I have found myself unable to reach even a gateway to a solution of the problem "what is life?", much less to synthesize it. But I understand now that minerals probably exert the greatest effect on the fundamental activities of living organisms. My understanding is based on the fact that after analyzing animals such as snakes, grasshoppers, earthworms and moles; pasture grasses such as kale; vegetables; and cereal grasses such as rice and barley, I found that they contain minerals as common components. Just burn an animal and a plant. You will get the same minerals from the ashes. All animals and plants, upon death, return to the earth like ash, and new lives are born by absorbing the minerals in the soil. In other words, living organisms are born and die with the minerals as an axis. This cycle is continuous like one ring."

This was the advice that led me on the path to Green Barley Essence. With it as a point of reference, I will begin with minerals as the primary of the five essential nutrients.

MINERALS—THE RING OF LIFE

In our minds we must consider ourselves quite removed from that moment billions of years ago when the first trace of life emerged on earth. But I believe that within our bodies we relive that drama of life creation millions of times every day, as the cells which form our tissue are reborn in countless succession in the life-sustaining chain. It is my belief that to promote this continuing act of rebirth, the elements from which life in matter arises must be as natural and balanced as they were at that pristine moment millions of years ago. For life to exist in any form, the most delicate of conditions must prevail.

What were those conditions like when life was first formed?

We can speculate that the earth at that time was covered with volcanoes spewing magma from deep within onto the earth's surface and into the oceans. Magma is a material which contains metallic elements, including alkali, metals and alkaline earth metals such as iron, magnesium, sodium, potassium and zinc.

When the earth's surface cooled, more mineral-laden soil was washed by rainwater into the ocean, giving rise to the saltiness of the oceans. The primitive ocean, however, probably contained more potassium but less sodium than today's oceans because potassium is more soluble in water than sodium.

Presumably, the first living thing took minerals from

the sea brine and gradually evolved to a higher living organism while repeating complex reactions. I conclude that we cannot but say that the minerals are the nucleus of physical life.

Plants arose far before the appearance of animals. An analysis of plants now on the earth shows that their cells contain more potassium than sodium. In other words, plant cells retain something close to the ionized condition of primitive sea brine, and no matter how much the cells may evolve, or the number of millennia that pass, the ion balance scarcely changes.

Is this irrelevant to the health of mankind? The answer is no. On the contrary, it relates to an important problem which present-day medicine and dietetics are neglecting.

When a living cell multiplies, it always does so by dividing into completely equal halves, retaining the original balance of minerals, like the primitive sea brine, no matter how complicated and diversified the organism becomes. Thus, even in the human being, as highly evolved an animal as he is, the nuclei of life still resemble the original sea brine in mineral content.

A greater understanding of this principal of natural balance might help us to be more conscious of what we put into our environment and into our bodies.

Balance and Maintenance of Minerals Is the Key to Health

Health means that the management of life activities within the body is normal. To maintain health, minerals such as potassium, magnesium and calcium are essential. Of these, potassium is of utmost importance. For potassium is contained inherently in the cells of a living organism to become a source of life activity. But the human habits of living and eating today do not maintain potassium and other minerals in favorable balance.

Dr. Fujita, who motivated me to go to young leaves of barley, believed that minerals are the essence of Chinese drugs. I must say I agree. He found evidence of this in the fact that these products are made mainly from the roots of grasses and barks of trees and retain their effectiveness even after being roasted or charred. Not a few of them are always charred before administration. If the essence of Chinese drugs was to be found in an organic substance such as ephedrine or morphine, no directions would be given to roast or char them prior to administration, as that would lead to the carbonization of the organic substances. Substances which can be obtained either in the raw, roasted, or charred state are none other than minerals.

Thus, I believe, we can conclude that the main purpose of Chinese drugs is to maintain the balance of minerals within our cells and to stimulate our life activities.

The human body, unlike plants, cannot draw needed minerals directly out of its environment or manufacture them from other substances. Our only source of these essential nutrients is in the food we eat. If foods of the proper mineral content are neglected, the body cannot prosper.

Table 8 illustrates that Green Barley Essence provides a higher quantity and better balance of minerals than any of the foods that are commonly valued for their nutrient qualities.

Figure 2 clearly shows that Green Barley Essence far surpasses other grains, protein-containing foods and vegetables in regard to mineral content. Since our present-day diet contains fewer minerals, the effectiveness of Green Barley Essence is all the more significant.

TABLE 8

Comparison of the Mineral Content of Green Barley Essence and
Several Popular Foods (milligrams per 100 grams)

	Food	Na	K	Ca	Mg	Fe	Cu	P	Mn	Zn
	GREEN BARLEY ESSENCE	**775**	**8,880**	**1,108**	**224.7**	**15.8**	**1.36**	**594**	**5.6**	**7.33**
Vegetables	Celery	28	278	37	9.6	1.4	0.11	45	-	-
	Lettuce	30	208	21	9.7	0.5	0.15	25	-	-
	Spinach	25	490	98	59.2	3.3	0.26	52	-	-
	Onion	10	137	40	7.6	0.5	0.08	26	-	-
	Tomato	3	288	3	11.0	0.2	0.10	18	-	-
	Cabbage	15	240	45	16.8	0.4	-	22	-	-
	Kale	-	-	225	-	-	-	67	-	-
	Comfrey	19	-	-	-	9.0	-	40	-	-
Fruits	Banana	8	348	5	41.9	0.4	0.16	23	-	-
	Apple	8	-	3	-	0.2	-	7	-	-
	Orange	4	-	14	-	0.2	-	12	-	-
Grains	Wheat flour	3	361	30	106.0	3.2	0.65	330	-	-
	Mixed wheat flour	3	132	118	1.9	1.9	0.17	111	-	-
	Refined rice (raw)	6	113	4	13.1	0.45	0.06	99	-	-
	Refined rice (cooked)	2	38	1	4.4	0.16	0.02	34	-	-
	Pressed barley	3	-	24	-	1.5	-	140	-	-
Dairy	Cow's milk	36	160	100	14.0	0.1	0.02	90	-	-
Fish	Salmon (canned)	500	320	170	29.8	1.2	0.05	320	-	-

Na: sodium   Fe: iron
K: potassium   Cu: copper
Ca: calcium   P: phosphorus
Mg: magnesium   Zn: zinc

Presented by Resource Research Association, Office of Science and Technology, and Japan Food Analysis Center

The King of Alkaline Foods

One of the important functions of minerals in our
bodies is to maintain the balance between acid and
alkaline. Should this balance be upset, the cell metabolism suffers, leading to conditions such as fatigue. Cells

maintain this balance by taking, consuming and discharging various minerals. Enzymes, the agents which make metabolism possible, work only when various minerals are dissolved as ions in the cell fluids. If the necessary minerals do not exist in an ionized condition, most of the enzymes lose their activity or have it reduced.

Potassium is an especially important mineral because it has a very high ionizing tendency. It is consumed incessantly within our bodies in the process of energy metabolism. When the potassium level falls too much, the osmotic pressure of the cell membrane is disrupted. To adjust the osmotic pressure, sodium and other ions take the place of potassium in the cells. As long as fresh potassium ions are continually supplied, there is no problem. But if the potassium supply fails, sodium increases above a healthy limit. Naturally, the balance of ions within the cell fluid is broken. Some enzymes continue to work, but others falter or completely stop functioning.

Our present-day diet tends to foster this condition because the proportion of acidic foods, such as meat, is large and the percentage of alkaline foods, primarily vegetables, is minor. Another cause is the consumption of reagent grade manufactured salt instead of the natural sea salt man used to use.

Green Barley Essence is the best food I have found to restore the acid-alkaline balance. It has an extremely high percentage of alkalinity, as shown in Figure 3. Spinach, the most popular alkaline food, has an alkalinity of 39.6, whereas the alkalinity of Green Barley Essence is as high as 66.4. Because of this high alkalinity, I should caution those who may be susceptible to over-alkalification. This condition, however, is rare and is extremely unlikely to become a problem unless Green

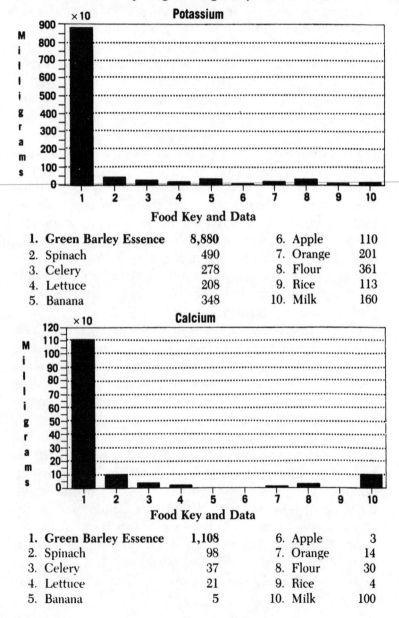

FIGURE 2
*Comparison of the Mineral Content of Green Barley Essence and
Several Foods by Weight (Milligrams per 100 Grams)*

Potassium

1. Green Barley Essence	8,880	6. Apple	110
2. Spinach	490	7. Orange	201
3. Celery	278	8. Flour	361
4. Lettuce	208	9. Rice	113
5. Banana	348	10. Milk	160

Calcium

1. Green Barley Essence	1,108	6. Apple	3
2. Spinach	98	7. Orange	14
3. Celery	37	8. Flour	30
4. Lettuce	21	9. Rice	4
5. Banana	5	10. Milk	100

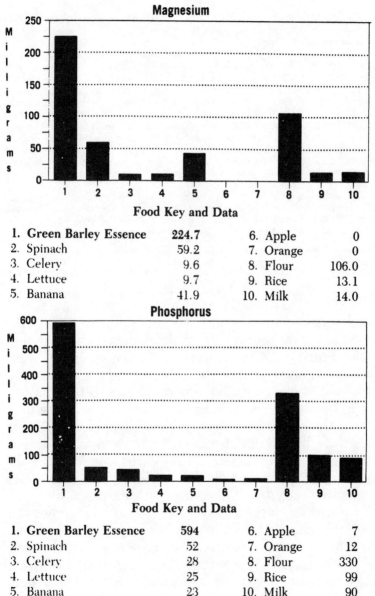

FIGURE 2
*Comparison of the Mineral Content of Green Barley Essence and
Several Foods by Weight (Milligrams per 100 Grams)*

Magnesium

1. Green Barley Essence	224.7	6. Apple	0
2. Spinach	59.2	7. Orange	0
3. Celery	9.6	8. Flour	106.0
4. Lettuce	9.7	9. Rice	13.1
5. Banana	41.9	10. Milk	14.0

Phosphorus

1. Green Barley Essence	594	6. Apple	7
2. Spinach	52	7. Orange	12
3. Celery	28	8. Flour	330
4. Lettuce	25	9. Rice	99
5. Banana	23	10. Milk	90

Note on Figure 2

The charts in Figure 2 illustrate the high concentration of important nutrients found in Green Barley Essence. Note that Figure 2 should not be interpreted as a comparison of the nutritional contents of foods in the quantities that constitute average servings. Most of the foods in these charts are typically eaten in amounts that weigh 50 to 150 grams. Because of its extremely high concentration and light weight, a result of almost all water being removed, Green Barley Essence is usually consumed by the teaspoon, an amount weighing approximately 2.5 grams. Even in this tiny amount, Green Barley Essence compares favorably in its content of a wide range of nutrients with other common foods eaten in significantly larger quantities.

Furthermore, there is really no way to assure that the foods found on the shopping market shelf will be equal in nutrient quality to those used in the standardized testing reflected in Figure 2. After picking, all fresh fruits and vegetables are subject to an aging process that robs them of essential vitamins and minerals, not to mention other active ingredients such as enzymes. Cooking even further erodes the nutrient content of these foods.

The nutrients specified for Green Barley Essence, on the other hand, are fixed by the spray-dry process soon after harvesting and remain stable a considerable time. Since Green Barley Essence is usually consumed in cool water, there is virtually no loss of nutrient content from that shown in Figure 2.

Barley Essence is consumed in much greater quantities than I suggested in the last chapter.

Acidic foods contain only small amounts of potassium and other minerals, and our environment is steadily increasing the deficiency of potassium. We must now take nutrition based primarily on minerals. It is no exaggeration to say that the imbalance of minerals within the cells causes a number of new diseases seen nowadays.

For example, hypocalcemia is a disease resulting from the reduction of calcium concentration in blood. It manifests itself in bone troubles, osteomalacia, abnormal excitation of nerves, or a disordered condition of the parathyroid gland. A similar disease, hypokalemia, results from a reduced potassium concentration in blood. Its symptoms include body languor, especially muscular fatigue, and can lead to paralysis in serious cases. Heart troubles may be caused by the same deficiencies. Furthermore, cirrhosis hepatitis is, in a sense, a disease associated with loss of potassium. Obviously, a defi-

FIGURE 3
*Milligrams of Alkaline Material Extracted from 100 Grams
of Various Foods*

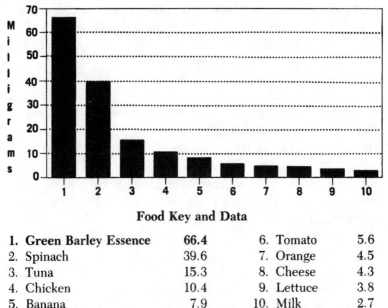

Food Key and Data

1. **Green Barley Essence**	**66.4**	6. Tomato	5.6
2. Spinach	39.6	7. Orange	4.5
3. Tuna	15.3	8. Cheese	4.3
4. Chicken	10.4	9. Lettuce	3.8
5. Banana	7.9	10. Milk	2.7

ciency of potassium causes a broad range of disease conditions. One of the most common may be debilitating fatigue.

Cause of Fatigue Is a Decrease in Potassium Level

The American magazine, *Medical Tribune*, reported that hypokalemia and hypocalcemia are induced also by the deficiency of a magnesium ion in body fluids. Experimental work by Dr. Maurice E. Sill of Cornell University has shown that when magnesium is deficient, the potassium or calcium level in body fluids decreases markedly, even if these minerals are being consumed in adequate quantity. Conversely, when proper magnesium absorption is restored, the calcium or potassium level also rises. As a result of this experimental work, Dr. Sill reported that "magnesium is indispensable for correctly mobilizing calcium from the bones and flesh, and storing potassium within the cells."

Let us now relate this discovery to our daily lives by showing how the common condition of fatigue is related to potassium deficiency. Fatigue comes in many varieites—the fatigue that follows vigorous physical exercise, the fatigue from tension or mental stress, or the fatigue from lack of sleep. These various kinds of fatigue may differ in the form of metabolism, but all share one phenomenon—the storing of sodium and the excretion of potassium.

Take for example, persons who habitually work at night. As shown in Figure 4, the blood of taxi drivers and long-distance truckdrivers clearly exhibits lower potassium levels and higher sodium levels than that present in the blood of general office clerks, who generally work in the daytime.

In another experiment, five healthy young men were asked to work eight hours at night and to sleep nine hours in the day. When this pattern, which is quite contrary to the ordinary sleep and work schedule, was continued four weeks with one holiday per week, a fairly marked increase in sodium and a fairly marked decrease in potassium were observed.

With regard to neurotic fatigue, I may cite an experiment in which a person was asked to monitor thirty instruments for hours on end without being informed which instrument would work at what time. The worker showed a clear decrease of potassium level and a clear

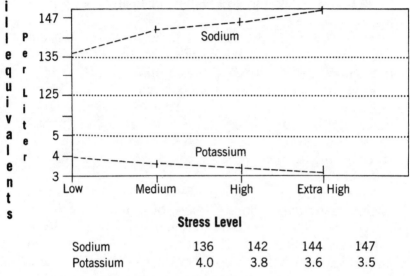

FIGURE 4

Change in the Balance of Sodium and Potassium Levels in the Blood Under Increasing Job Stress

	Low	Medium	High	Extra High
Sodium	136	142	144	147
Potassium	4.0	3.8	3.6	3.5

Low stress:	Office work
Medium stress:	Irregular working hours
High stress:	Taxi driver
Extra high stress:	Long-distance truck driver

(Analyzed by Hajime Saito. Institute of Labor Science. Japan.)

increase in sodium level in his blood on an on-duty day as compared with an off-duty day.

Similar results were obtained after physical exercise or labor under intense heat. One interesting report was made by Dr. Richard L. Westerman in the National Conference on Athletic Medicine held in 1970 in Indiana. He reported that athletes could prevent heatstroke by taking potassium in addition to the salt and water now customarily given. The sodium level becomes excessive within the athlete who has reached a high level of fatigue and this causes disordered conditions such as heatstroke. Dr. Westerman recommended supplying 20 to 25 mg of potassium and water per liter of body fluid lost by sweating.

As is clear from the above data and reports, tension and muscular fatigue are induced by the excretion of potassium and the build-up of sodium.

What happens to those who continually follow a diet deficient in potassium? Since the body has a self-defending system, there will be an effort to store potassium within the cells. If complete loss of potassium is threatened, the body tries to prevent secretion of potassium.

As a consequence, our bodies are forced to stop all strong muscular exercise. Exertions of the brain or nerves, which consume even greater energy than physical labor, become dull. This in turn causes the body to stop releasing potassium, and results in sleepiness and languidness. You may have experienced this yourself. If so, it was at a time when the potassium level in your body decreased markedly and the body had stopped releasing it. If you noticed this and took potassium, the cells would regain vigor and resume energy metabolism.

Cattle and horses, which feed only on grasses, have long been known for their ability to work to exhaustion, then rest and, after feeding on grasses, come to life again. This is due presumably to potassium and many other nutrients contained in abundance in the grasses which they eat. Why should humans not enjoy the same revitalization by taking Green Barley Essence?

Now let us consider the second essential nutrient, vitamins.

VITAMINS—GUARDIANS OF GOOD HEALTH

While almost everyone in the developed world receives an adequate supply of vitamins—either in the natural form or through enriched processed foods—to prevent the notorious consequences of malnutrition such as scurvy and beriberi, many health enthusiasts today have taken an interest in extremely large doses of vitamins to retard the aging process, enhance their sexuality or enjoy more energy.

This rapidly growing field of dietetic study from which I believe much valuable information will come, emphasizes the importance of supplementing the diet with a food such as Green Barley Essence, which is a prolific source of vitamins.

Table 9 and Figure 5 show that Green Barley Essence contains abundant vitamins. Our health problems would be significantly reduced if these vitamins could be taken sufficiently in our daily diet. However, this is actually not the case. For example, vitamin C, contained in crushed raw radish is reduced by half after about five minutes' exposure, and more than 70 percent of it decomposes in about twenty minutes. Vitamins B1 and B2 in foods also decrease drastically in quantity when they are cooked for a long time. But if you take even a spoonful of Green Barley Essence dissolved in water, you will be able to gain abundant vitamins in active form (that is, in natural form).

Clearly, Green Barley Essence contains vitamins in quantities which far surpass those of other foods.

Needless to say, vitamins are important for health. Vitamins impart activity to enzymes within the body, thus promoting metabolism. Vitamins also assist the body in maintaining health against a variety of well-known diseases and conditions. Nutritional science has

TABLE 9
Comparison of the Vitamin Content of Green Barley Essence and Several Popular Foods

	Food	Carotene I.U.	B1 (mg)	B2 (mg)	B6 (mg)	C (mg)	E (mg)	H Biotin (μ)	Folic Acid (μ)	Panto-thenic Acid*	Nico-tinic Acid*	Chloro-phyll (mg)	Cho-line (mg)
	Green Barley Essence	52,000	1.29	2.75	0.03	329	-	48.0	640	2.48	10.6	149	260
	Celery	0	1.03	1.02	0.10	10	0.5	0.1	7	0.40	0.4	-	-
	Lettuce	200	0.06	0.06	0.07	5	0.5	0.7	20	0.10	0.2	-	-
	Spinach	8,000	0.12	0.30	0.10	100	-	0.1	80	0.30	1.0	-	-
Vege-tables	Onion	20	0.03	0.02	0.10	10	0.3	0.9	10	0.10	0.2	-	-
	Tomato	400	0.08	0.03	0.10	20	0.4	1.2	5	0.05	0.8	-	-
	Cabbage	100	0.08	0.05	-	50	-	-	-	-	0.5	-	-
	Kale	10,000	0.15	0.33	-	126	-	-	-	-	-	-	-
	Comfrey	9,800	0.77	2.20	-	60	-	-	-	-	1.0	-	-
	Banana	200	0.03	0.05	0.30	10	0.4	-	10	0.20	0.5	-	-
	Apple	45	0.01	0.01	-	55	-	-	-	-	0.1	-	-
Fruits	Orange (fresh)	120	0.09	0.02	-	50	-	-	-	-	1.0	-	-
	Orange (concentrate)	20	-	-	-	3	-	-	-	-	1.0	-	-
	Wheat flour	-	0.30	0.10	0.40	-	2.6	5.0	35	4.50	4.5	-	-
	Mixed wheat flour	-	-	-	0.10	-	1.7	0.6	14	0.80	-	-	-
Grains	Refined rice (raw)	-	-	-	0.30	-	0.4	3.0	10	6.60	-	-	-
	Refined rice (cooked)	-	-	-	-	-	-	-	-	-	-	-	-
	Pressed barley	-	0.18	0.07	-	-	-	-	-	-	2.5	-	-
Dairy	Cow's Milk	20	0.04	0.15	0.04	2	-	2.0	0.3	0.35		-	-
Fish	Salmon (canned)	-	0.02	0.12	0.03	-	-	10.0	5.0	0.50	-	-	20.1

*milligrams

Presented by Resource Research Association, Office of Science and Technology, and Japan Food Analysis Center.

well documented these specific conditions and the quantities of vitamins required for effective prevention. This information is widely published in literature available in most health food stores.

As I have already mentioned, however, to be effective for the health, these must be natural vitamins, not synthetic ones.

Recently, vitamin E has attracted considerable interest as a possible inhibitor of certain diseases. Many pharmaceuticals and health foods containing high units of vitamin E are now being marketed. This trend reminds me of the excitement generated by high-unit vitamin B1 tablets, and the subsequent abuse of high-unit vitamin C preparations for their alleged effectiveness against pigment deposition and rough skin. Soon, the side effects caused by high dosages of these high-unit synthetic vitamins put a curb on their manufacture and sale. I fear that high-dose administration of vitamin E will cause a similar reaction.

Even vitamins, as necessary as they are, can break the balance of a living body if excessively consumed.

This is so, I believe, because, as previously stated, the human body is made of a balance of inorganic and organic properties. Adverse effects can be caused by the ingestion in large quantities of anything but natural food of a balanced organic-inorganic nature. High dosages of chemical pharmaceuticals throw off the balance of the body, leading inevitably to side effects.

In view of this, I conclude that natural green vegetables are the only source of vitamins which can be taken for a long period of time without risk of side effects.

In addition to being natural, these vegetables must be grown according to the standards I have described earlier. It has been found recently that because vegetables are now grown mostly by forced cultivation techniques, they have much lower contents of minerals and vitamins than those grown naturally. If we eat only such vegetables, vitamins and minerals in our bodies will become deficient.

FIGURE 5
Comparison of the Vitamin Content of Green Barley Essence and Several Foods by Weight (Milligrams per 100 Grams)

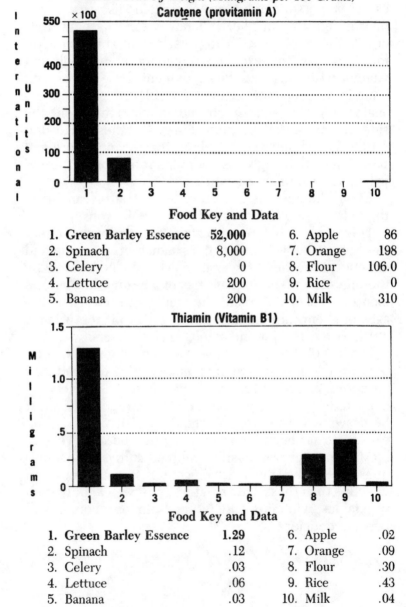

Carotene (provitamin A)

International Units × 100

Food Key and Data

1.	Green Barley Essence	52,000	6.	Apple	86
2.	Spinach	8,000	7.	Orange	198
3.	Celery	0	8.	Flour	106.0
4.	Lettuce	200	9.	Rice	0
5.	Banana	200	10.	Milk	310

Thiamin (Vitamin B1)

Milligrams

Food Key and Data

1.	Green Barley Essence	1.29	6.	Apple	.02
2.	Spinach	.12	7.	Orange	.09
3.	Celery	.03	8.	Flour	.30
4.	Lettuce	.06	9.	Rice	.43
5.	Banana	.03	10.	Milk	.04

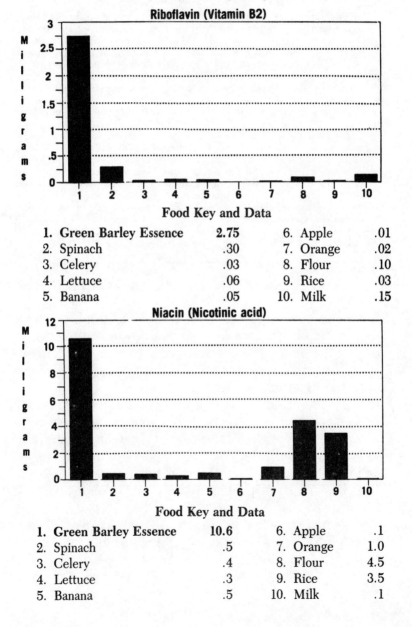

FIGURE 5

Comparison of the Vitamin Content of Green Barley Essence and Several Foods by Weight (Milligrams per 100 Grams)

Riboflavin (Vitamin B2)

Food Key and Data

1. Green Barley Essence	2.75	6. Apple	.01
2. Spinach	.30	7. Orange	.02
3. Celery	.03	8. Flour	.10
4. Lettuce	.06	9. Rice	.03
5. Banana	.05	10. Milk	.15

Niacin (Nicotinic acid)

Food Key and Data

1. Green Barley Essence	10.6	6. Apple	.1
2. Spinach	.5	7. Orange	1.0
3. Celery	.4	8. Flour	4.5
4. Lettuce	.3	9. Rice	3.5
5. Banana	.5	10. Milk	.1

Note on Figure 5

The charts in Figure 5 illustrate the high concentration of important nutrients found in Green Barley Essence. Take note that Figure 5 should not be interpreted as a comparison of the nutritional contents of foods in the quantities that constitute average servings. Most of the foods in these charts are typically eaten in amounts that weigh 50 to 150 grams. Because of its extremely high concentration and light weight, a result of almost all water being removed, Green Barley Essence is usually consumed by the teaspoon, an amount weighing approximately 2.5 grams. Even in this tiny amount, Green Barley Essence compares favorably in its content of a wide range of nutrients with other common foods eaten in significantly larger quantities.

Furthermore, there is really no way to assure that the foods found on the shopping market shelf will be equal in nutrient quality to those used in the standardized testing reflected in Figure 5. After picking, all fresh fruits and vegetables are subject to an aging process that robs them of essential vitamins and minerals, not to mention other active ingredients such as enzymes. Cooking even further erodes the nutrient content of these foods.

The nutrients specified for Green Barley Essence, on the other hand, are fixed by the spray-dry process soon after harvesting and remain stable a considerable time. Since Green Barley Essence is usually consumed in cool water, there is virtually no loss of nutrient content from that shown in Figure 5.

PROTEINS—BUILDING BLOCKS OF LIFE

I believe it is common for people to think of meat, fish, milk and poultry as high sources of protein, without giving the same consideration to the protein content of plants. This is a false assumption. Many plants are high in protein content, as I already pointed out in the previous chapter. Among them, young green barley leaves are highest. As Table 7 demonstrated, protein comprises about 45 percent by weight of the ingredients of Green Barley Essence, representing its largest single component. To pursue this comparison, the content by weight of protein is only 10 percent in wheat flour, a striking difference.

A significant consideration in the comparison of protein foods is the complexity of the protein molecules that reach the digestive tract. Some protein molecules are very difficult for the human body to break down and assimilate. Others, often referred to as lightweight protein molecules or polypeptides, can be very easy for the body to handle and use. Green Barley Essence is rich in those lightweight proteins.

Perhaps of even more importance is the relationship between usable protein and crude protein. Usable protein is related to the proportions of the various amino acids in the food supply. The body requires amino acids in specific proportions to build tissue. If a food is low in one or more of them, the body will be unable to use the other amino acids fully. In the case of Green Barley Essence, it is rich in lightweight protein molecules (45%) of which 90 percent is usable.

Because of the interest in the subject of specific amino acids and the related topic of fatty acids, extracts from the green leaves of barley were analyzed for fatty acid and amino acid compositions. The results, shown in the following Tables 10 and 11, demonstrate that these extracts contain large amounts of essential fatty acids such as linoleic acid and linolenic acid (not synthesized in the human body), and also essential amino acids such as valine, leucine, isoleucine, phenylalanine, threonine and methionine in a well-balanced state.

In conclusion, I would suggest that Green Barley Essence actually represents a stronger source of protein than foods such as meat and milk because it does not come burdened with the fat and grease associated with those foods.

CHLOROPHYLL—STORED ENERGY OF THE SUN

A subject which may need more introduction than proteins, minerals and vitamins is the beneficial function of chlorophyll in the diet. An examination of the chemical structure of chlorophyll may help.

TABLE 10
Breakdown of Fatty Acid Composition in Green Barley Essence
(Early Internode Growing Stage)

Capric acid	0.1%
Lauric acid	1.5
Myristic acid	2.5
Palmitic acid	18.0
Zoomaric acid	3.5
Stearic acid	1.5
Oleic acid	2.0
Linoleic acid	8.9
Linolenic acid	49.9
Arachidic acid	0.4
Erucic acid	0.6
Unidentifiable acids	11.1

Under examination, the cells of the human body are much like those of green leaves. For example, the composition of electrolytes (minerals) is much the same for both.

My interest in this comparison focuses on the extraordinary similarity between chlorophyll in green leaves and human blood. In chemical structure chlorophyll and blood would appear to be twins. The only difference, as shown in Diagram 1, is that chlorophyll contains magnesium (Mg) bonded in its structure, whereas hemoglobin contains iron (Fe). We may well say that the fluid in green leaves is the blood of grasses or trees. Conversely, I venture to maintain that the green blood can become red blood in man.

In 1949, *Reader's Digest* magazine carried a special article entitled "Mysterious Power of Chlorophyll." Chlorophyll then came into vogue, and also attracted medi-

TABLE 11

Free Amino Acid Composition in the Protein of Green Barley
Essence (Early Internode Growing Stage)

Amino acid nitrogen	0.58%
Tryptophan	0.66
Glycine	2.32
Alanine	3.12
Valine	2.59
Leucine	3.38
Isoleucine	1.91
Proline	2.10
Phenylalanine	2.22
Tyrosine	0.82
Serine	1.44
Threonine	1.75
Cystine	0.32
Methionine	0.19
Arginine	2.12
Histidine	0.76
Lysine	2.33
Aspartic acid	3.98
Glutamic acid	4.94

cal attention. For some time, chlorophyll was added to products from medicines to toothpastes.

But one problem exists. The chlorophyll then reported on and used was not natural chlorophyll. It was a substance called copper chlorophyllin sodium obtained by decomposing natural chlorophyll and binding a copper ion to it. As shown in Diagram 1, natural chlorophyll contains a magnesium atom as a central atom.

Why was such a product synthesized? The answer is that chlorophyll is a substance which is chemically very unstable. It loses its green immediately upon exposure

Diagram 1
Structural Formulas of Human Blood and Chlorophyll

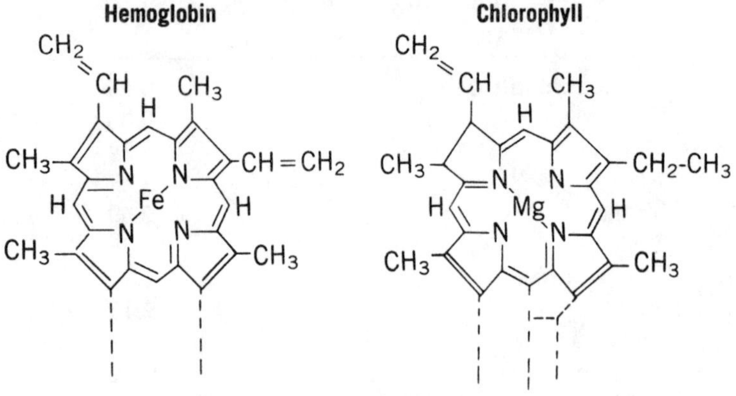

Hemoglobin

Chlorophyll

to sunlight or drying, and it also loses its biochemical activity. Artificial chlorophyll having a copper ion bonded to it is readily soluble in water and retains its bluish green whether exposed to sunlight or treated otherwise. This is like a colored soft drink; a false thing looks more real than a real thing. But it cannot be called chlorophyll. Moreover, the artificial chlorophyll is scarcely absorbable within the body, and so has no effect when we ingest it. Ironically, that makes artificial chlorophyll all the more safe. For if it were readily absorbable, it would surely be toxic too.

The evidence from one clinical experiment showed that administration of copper chlorophyllin sodium by injection gave rise to such side effects as anemia and nausea. For this reason, no injecting preparation containing chlorophyllin has been manufactured for sale.

Since these facts were made clear, claims for the beneficial effects of copper chlorophyllin sodium were withdrawn. Today, only its deodorant activity is recognized. According to the Japanese Law of Food Sanitation of the Ministry of Welfare and Health, it is designated not as a pharmaceutical but as a synthetic colorant.

Natural chlorophyll is produced by naturally growing plants and is a source of their life activity. We cannot gain chlorophyll from any source other than the leaves of plants.

Artificial chlorophyll results from the bonding of a copper ion, but natural chlorophyll has a magnesium ion as a central atom. This is a decisive difference between chlorophyll and copper chlorophyllin regarding their absorbability in the human body.

At one time it was thought that chlorophyll, as a polymer with very firm bonding, could not be absorbed through the intestinal tract. In an attempt to determine the digestive mechanism of chlorophyll in the intestinal tract, I performed various experiments. Based on the fact that chlorophyll is soluble in fat particles and that fat particles are believed to be absorbed directly from the intestinal tract, I imagined that chlorophyll would be absorbed from the intestinal tract in a form dissolved in fat particles. Mice were fed chlorophyll, and examined by an electron microscope. It seems that the polymeric chlorophyll was fairly well absorbed. But I could not ascertain in what form it was absorbed.

I later located a research report of an American worker which said that when a high frequency wave was applied to chlorophyll, the polymeric chlorophyll was split off. According to technical phraseology, this process is called ring opening. If you refer back to the chemical structure of chlorophyll, you can see that its bonding forms circles. These are called porphyrin rings, and ring opening is the process of splitting these rings.

Although chlorophyll in polymer form may not be absorbable, the ring-opened chlorophyll can be easily absorbed. What does it become then? It will naturally be absorbed through the lymphatic vessels or blood vessels.

I would like to suggest the possibility that the chlorophyll absorbed by the lymphatic fluid and blood in the ring-opened form will again be formed into the porphyrin rings, not through a magnesium ion this time but through an iron ion as a central metabolic ion as a result of a reaction within the living body.

What is the significance of this reasoning? As you can see from the previous diagram, if the magnesium ion is removed from the molecular structure of chlorophyll, and an iron ion is attached instead, it becomes the structural formula of hemoglobin. Thus, the conclusion drawn from my reasoning is that the green blood of the plant can become the red blood of man.

Further studies must be done to establish this as a scientific fact. For the time being, I will call it my scientific romance. And I am fairly confident that such scientific substantiation will be established some day.

When a solution of chlorophyll is exposed to sunlight, it completely absorbs sunlight and turns nearly black. This is the phenomenon of chlorophyll storing solar energy. Within the plant cells, the stored energy is utilized for new organic syntheses required for life activities. When the chlorophyll which has absorbed sunlight is examined in the dark, it looks reddish-violet. This fluorescence is caused by the release of stored energy.

As previously stated, the ionized state of man's cellular fluids is very similar to that of a plant. The substance which becomes a source of life for plants cannot be ineffective for man.

In Japan there is a typical folk remedy in which an injury is cured by applying a juice squeezed from the leaves of wormwood to the injured site. This promptly stops the bleeding. This is also due to the activity of chlorophyll.

ENZYMES—REGULATORS OF THE BODY

Modern science has made it clear that all chemical changes within the cells of man are performed by the action of enzymes. It has also been found that minerals have much to do with the activities of enzymes. In this sense, minerals can be said to be enzymes for the enzymes. Let us now see in greater detail what enzymes are.

Briefly stated, enzymes are catalysts for chemical changes in the living body. Various syntheses and decompositions occur at considerable speeds within our cells and digestive tract and other organs of our body. It is the enzymes which perform and promote these reactions under normal conditions.

Enzymes are required to decompose and digest the foods we eat. Similarly, a gas exchange inside the lungs sends the air we breathe into the blood and cells. This gas exchange would be impossible without enzymes. When we get an injury, enzymes act to stop bleeding and create new cells. Enzymes are also involved in moving our hands and legs, and even in the process of thinking.

Our body functions normally only in the presence of enzymes. If the enzymes were lost, all functions of our body would fail. Let us now look into the activities of these important enzymes more closely.

When we take a bite of food, an enzyme called pytalin immediately comes from the salivary gland. The enzymes serve to convert starch to maltose. In the stomach, an enzyme called pepsin acts to decompose protein. In the small intestine such enzymes as trypsin, elastase and lipase act to decompose amino acids to proteins and fats to fatty acids. These decomposition products are absorbed by various parts of our body. Enzymes are also involved in synthesizing proteins from amino acids to make muscle.

More than 3,000 Varieties of Enzymes

Until the middle of the eighteenth century, it was quite unknown in what form foods were absorbed from the digestive tracts. Towards the end of the eighteenth century, Spallanzani of Italy succeeded in extracting the gastric juice of a bird using a metal tube. He found that when this juice was put into a tube and caused to act on a piece of meat kept at the temperature of the human body, the meat was dissolved.

This great discovery formed the basis of enzymology. A French scientist named Debrunfant succeeded in an experiment of saccharifying starch with wheat germ as an agent in 1823. In 1933, an enzyme in the wheat germ which promoted the decomposing action of starch was successfully extracted. This enzyme is diastase.

Through succeeding discoveries, over 3,000 enzymes have now been identified and out of them 300 have been extracted as pure crystals. It is quite probable that many more enzymes are working in every part of the body. We expect that new enzymes will be discovered year by year.

No doubt, many of those enzymes are applicable to the treatment of diseases. Digestive enzymes typified by pepsin, discovered in the eighteenth century, were already used for treating patients with poor digestion some twenty years after their discovery.

Enzymes have the property of acting only on specific

substances; that is, they catalyze only specific reactions. Under different conditions, they fail to act. In recent years, the complex activities of numerous enzymes within our bodies have gradually been elucidated, and the utmost importance of enzymes in life activities has been recognized. Much remains to be learned. We can now safely say that a substantial supply of enzymes is needed in the diet.

Green Barley Essence contains numerous enzymes. The 1979 General Meeting of the Japanese Society of Pharmaceutical Science reported finding more than twenty enzymes in Green Barley Essence. In addition, many researchers throughout the world have ascertained that the leaves of higher plants, including cereal grasses, contain a number of enzymes such as cytochrome oxidase (an oxidation-reduction enzyme required for cell respiration), peroxidase (an enzyme to decompose hydrogen peroxide), catalase, fatty acid oxidase (an enzyme to oxidize fatty acid) and transhydrogenase. When these enzymes become weak, the decomposition of fats within the body does not proceed smoothly, causing build-up of fats within the body and, consequently, weight gain.

Cytochrome oxidase, peroxidase and catalase are contained in very great amounts in red blood cells and white blood cells. It is said that they are extremely low in content in cancerous cells. This might mean that the application of catalase to cancerous cells is likely to result in the inhibition of cancer. Also, these enzymes can decompose toxic substances within our body. Transhydrogenase is an enzyme which performs an important function with regard to the muscular tissue of the heart.

In addition to those mentioned, it has also been found that Green Barley Essence contains nitrogen oxyreductase, aspartate, amino transferase and many other enzymes. I believe that further study will turn up thousands of enzymes in Green Barley Essence. Hence, it may well be called a treasure house of enzymes.

In the production technique I developed for Green Barley Essence, the temperature stays at about human body temperature. The natural enzymes in the barley leaves would be destroyed at any higher temperature.

In summary, minerals (especially potassium, calcium and magnesium), vitamins, proteins, chlorophyll and enzymes are the keys to health. Together, they maintain our cells in a healthy condition and work to correct any abnormal condition that occurs. They do it not like drugs, which are foreign matter within the body, but serve to invigorate natural activities within the body.

As I have said before, the use of drugs and synthetic food supplements, in an attempt to regulate the body's activities and supply a surplus of these five essential elements, can too easily lead to imbalance and harmful side effects. Only when fed in natural and balanced form, as is available in Green Barley Essence, can these five essential elements perform the work they are meant to do. Inside the body, these nutrients work together in an extremely complex pattern of interrelationships, the effects of one depending on the presence of the others.

From the standpoint of enzymes, for example, the power of each of the enzymes cannot be exerted unless there exist various minerals such as iron, copper, zinc and sodium.

Health can only be maintained when enzymes work together with minerals. Cytochrome oxidase, an enzyme which catalyzes oxidation reduction, contains one copper ion and one iron ion in its chemical structure. SOD, an enzyme which prevents aging of cells, cannot exhibit its inherent activity without minerals such as zinc or copper. In other words, it is only when the body contains minerals in a well-balanced state that as many as three thousand and several hundred enzymes can perform harmonized metabolism.

In the remaining chapters of my book, I will begin to discuss in more detail how these five great constituents of Green Barley Essence work within the body to invigorate the cells, maintain health and prevent disease. As a prelude to this, I would again refer to the famous saying of Hippocrates, the father of medicine, whom I quoted earlier: "A disease should be cured naturally by man's own power . . ."

What does Green Barley Essence have to do with that? As I shall now describe, Green Barley Essence is the perfect fuel to sustain "man's own power" in its quest for good health.

CHAPTER 5

RELATION OF ABNORMAL CONSTITUTION TO DISEASE

THE HUMAN BODY: A SUPREME VEHICLE
FOR HEALTH

MY TEACHER, Dr. Fujita, once warned that new diseases will increase in the future because of the hazardous effects of synthetic drugs. That predication has already come true.

In May 1975, the Japanese Ministry of Welfare and Health added several new diseases to its already long list of difficult-to-cure diseases.

The list now comprises: periarteritis nodosa, colitis ulcerosa, pulmonary emphysema, aortitis syndrome, Buerger's disease, pemphigus, myelocerebellar degeneration, juvenile hypertension, essential hypertension, Crohn's disease, portal hypertension, hepatic angiosarcoma, intrahepatic cholestasis, Sjögren's syndrome, amyloidosis, idiopathic non-suppurative osteonecrosis, ossification of the posterior longitudinal ligaments and quadriceps contracture. You may be surprised by names you have never heard of. But they exist around you.

In addition, various "modern diseases," such as cancer, cerebral hemorrhage, heart diseases, liver diseases and neurogenic diseases are on the increase. There are also

childhood obesity, shortsightedness, hernia of the inter-
vertebral disc, aging of the skin and feeble constitution
to detract from the picture of a "healthy" human race.

I understand that in the United States, where the
diet consists mainly of meat, about half of the national
population is suffering from constipation and about 3,000
kinds of drugs are on sale for its treatment. Constipation may eventually cause diseases of the internal organs and aging of the skin.

In addition, diseases which we never heard of ten
years ago are now increasing in number, such as intersti-
tial inflammation, also known as collagen disease, myas-
thenia, Behçet's syndrome, multiple sclerosis, Addison's
disease, Parkinson's disease, Ménière's disease and
Kaschin-Beck disease. And more.

The causes of these diseases are mostly unclear, and
no decisive therapeutic methods have been found. I
believe the the place to look for a cause is in the
deteriorated constitution of the human race, a direct
result of failing nutrition.

Preventive medicine intended for improving the constitution of our body is more necessary now than in any
past period in man's history.

The present situation is miserable. Many hospitals
are being built, and a growing number of persons are
engaged in medical therapy, and pharmaceuticals are
being manufactured in greater quantities every year.
Despite this, the number of the diseased does not at all
decrease. Physicians must first give their attention to
those already diseased, and so cannot afford time for a
study of prophylactic medicine which leads to the prevention of disease. It is left to us to do the best we can
to prevent disease for ourselves. How must this be
done?

The first thing we must do is reexamine our exaggerated reliance on synthetic drugs. Wherever possible, we should reduce our use of pharmaceuticals to treat every ailment that comes along. Instead, we should build a form of natural protection by maintaining nutritionally healthy bodies.

To understand this, it would perhaps help to distinguish between two views on the nature of the living body.

The first view, which is commonly held by those who practice Western medicine, describes the body as a feeble, worn-down machine that is constantly vulnerable to attack by something outside it called disease. According to this view, once that disease gets inside the body, it can only be eliminated with the help of potent synthetic agents or, in extreme cases, by surgically removing diseased tissue.

I prefer to think of the living body as the supreme vehicle of good health. From the resources outside it, the body feeds its cells and removes toxins to create a healthy, dynamic physical form. The disease that others view as an assault from the outside is really nothing more than a lapse or breach of the processes within the body. Part of what keeps the body in form is the very spirit of life itself. When this spirit fails, the body fails with it, leading to disease.

Just as some people seem naturally more endowed with this life spirit than others, there are people who have an extraordinary ability to prosper physically, with no apparent harm, under an extreme deficiency of the nutrient resources that are required to keep the body in form. More often, though, the fact is that the person who seems to be well-nourished and healthy enough is actually barely sustaining life with a half-starved, toxin-laden environment within the tissues of the body where the life force is at work.

When the effects of this self-denial begin to show up as malaise, fatigue, anemia and finally disease, the common reaction is to "attack" the problem with artificial solutions such as synthetic vitamin and mineral preparations, aspirin, antibiotics or more radical treatments such as adrenocortical steroids or radioactive therapy.

While these techniques may show some temporary relief, their long-term effects are to further undermine the body's own dynamic process by adding to the burden of toxins the body must remove, while denying the natural nutrients the body requires to perform this function.

To be truly healthy we must not rely on synthetic pharmaceuticals alone. We must supply our bodies with the five great constituents which I outlined in the previous chapter.

Hazardous Effects of Synthetic Drugs

First of all, it should be understood that when a living body is operating soundly, substances which it needs are formed naturally within the body, and it is insignificant and unnecessary to supply foreign matter from outside. If essential substances with the body are lacking, it is necessary to replenish them to some extent. But sources of supply must be raw natural substances. These substances should be natural foods plentiful in enzymes and minerals. For our health can be seriously damaged by attempts to load the nutritional system artificially.

In this regard, I have already mentioned the great effectiveness of chlorophyll and the ineffectiveness and hazardous nature of artificial chlorophyll, chlorophyllin. The importance of potassium is equally recognized in the medical field. A drug containing potassium chloride is sometimes used for therapeutic purposes. However, a living body necessarily develops an abnormal reaction against such a synthetic drug. Side effects reported with the use of potassium chloride include the appearance of tumors in the large intestine. This, of course, would not occur were the potassium to be taken in a natural form such as in green barley leaf juice, which is a food.

The same can be said with regard to sodium glutamate or lysine. Certainly, experimental data are available which demonstrate the favorable effects of glutamic acid and lysine on the activity of the brain. With this information, these substances have come into use in large quantities and, predictably, it has been discovered that such use of them may cause side effects.

Similarly, it is dangerous to take proteins in high concentrations simply on the ground that proteins are nutritionally very important. To take a great quantity of only one type of substance will usually lead to trouble.

The relation of the body to those ingredients essential for our subsistence is that of a key to a keyhole. Artificial substances and synthetic drugs may bring about temporary effects, but do not fit in the keyholes. Let me give an example of what I mean by this.

Generally, adrenocortical hormones are antiinflammatory agents which are used extensively throughout the world. Derivatives of the adrenocortical hormones are called steroidal agents. Long ago, the World Health Organization warned that steroidal agents should not be used except in special or emergency cases. Physicians, however, seem to have no hesitation about using them for treating inflammation.

Steroidal agents are used orally for the treatment of diseases of internal organs, such as gastritis and hepatitis, and externally or parenterally for treatment of dermatitis, chronic eczema and burns. However, on long-term administration, steroidal agents cause a loss of natural hormonal secretions which protect against inflammation. The hormone-producing organs are rather lazy, and once they sense the external application of hormones, they stop producing hormones by themselves. Thus ironically, when large quantities of hormones are given from outside the body, the adrenal glands lose their ability to produce those hormones by themselves.

When administration of an adrenocortical hormone is stopped, the disease immediately gets worse. Thus, hormone treatments are begun again. If this is repeated, the secretion of hormones becomes weaker and the condition of the body is disturbed, resulting in peripheral abnormalities including "moon face" and loss of vigor. It is even said that many of those who habitually take an adrenocortical hormone commit suicide.

To remedy this condition, an activating agent is necessary which invigorates the adrenal glands themselves and promotes hormonal secretion. Green Barley Essence is very effective as such an activating agent. With long-term use of Green Barley Essence, its polypeptide-like enzymes act on the adrenal glands to promote hormonal secretion.

Promotes Mobility of the Intestinal Tract

If sufficient potassium is not supplied when our bodies issue a warning in the form of fatigue, what will happen?

This is the beginning of a disease. Fatigue is the first warning that the ion balance within the cells is out of order. If this condition continues, the cells will become unable to perform their inherent functions.

Hypokalemia also leads to gastric troubles such as nausea. This is because the deficiency of potassium culminates in stopping the intestinal tract movement.

This effect was shown in a rather grisly experiment in which the intestinal tract of a rabbit was removed and all its potassium extracted. The movement of the intestinal tract came to an almost complete stop in 45 minutes. But when potassium is restored, the movement begins again in 15 minutes.

Because of its high content of potassium, Green Barley Essence brings about good evacuation, which is not an insignificant form of preventive medicine.

These are but two examples of the way in which Green Barley Essence works as a preventive medicine by promoting the healthy condition which is natural to the living body.

It has now been nearly twenty years since I first introduced Green Barley Essence to the public of Japan. During this span of time I have learned of its power to alleviate literally hundreds of aggravations and health problems which previously resisted traditional treatment. This knowledge, I am pleased to say, comes from the thousands of people who have experienced relief and have written to tell me about it.

CHAPTER 6 ═══════════════════

RELIEF FOR MANY ILLS

GREEN BARLEY ESSENCE HELPS RESTORE LOST HEALTH: TESTIMONIAL LETTERS

I ORIGINALLY INTRODUCED Green Barley Essence with the modest purpose of presenting it to the public as a healthy convenience food to take the place of the unhealthy junk foods which have come to occupy such a large percentage of the modern diet. While my intention was to promote better health through the method of preventive nutrition and while I believed that Green Barley Essence would restore health to those damaged by synthetic drug treatments, I did not at first conceive of it as a drug or medicine intended to treat a specific ailment.

Thousands of letters from people who used Green Barley Essence have now expanded my estimation of its value. Many of these letters provide testimony to its powerful curative effect on ailments in people who had given up on receiving any benefit from traditional methods of treatment.

Some of the letters which have come to my Association of Green and Health are reproduced here to give you an idea of the many symptoms of ill health against which Green Barley Essence has proven effective.

Of course, these letters represent the simple, unsolicited response of the public, not controlled scientific test cases, and must be read in that light.

Asthma and Eczema

From Miss Michiko Nogami, seventeen years old, Takamatsu City, Kagawa-ken:

"I am a seventeen-year-old girl. I have been suffering from asthma since childhood, and also frequently from eczema. I have made many visits to my town's asthma clinic, with little benefit.

"Then I heard of Green Barley Essence and immediately tried it. After taking it a little more than one month, I found myself free of eczema. I also noticed that the attacks of asthma were reduced and even when I had an attack of it, the symptoms were milder.

"After taking Green Barley Essence for six months, I scarcely have any attacks and I find my skin has become increasingly beautiful. I can't believe what has happened."

Obesity

From Mrs. Fumiko Yoshioka, sixty years old, Yahata-Ku, Kitakyushu-Shi:

"I am short in height, but weigh far too much at 65 kg (145 lbs). I have high blood pressure and get considerable shoulder stiffness. Hoping to cure this condition, I began to try Green Barley Essence after reading about it in a book on natural foods.

"I once took an antihypertensive which is supposed to be good for losing weight. But I stopped taking it and stick only to Green Barley Essence and other natural foods which seem more effective. I now rarely have shoulder stiffness and my weight has decreased to 60 kg (134 lbs). I'm now trying hard to lose more weight."

Beautification, Skin Rejuvenation

From Mrs. Miyoko Hashizume, forty-four years old, Kita-ku, Osaka:

"My interest raised by an article in a certain women's magazine, I began to take Green Barley Essence about six months ago. At that time I had a poor complexion, dull and dark in color. Now my complexion has become vivid and fair, despite the fact that I am using the same cosmetics as before. All my friends have been surprised by the change and my husband says that I seem to have become younger."

Pimples and Rough Skin

From Miss Noriko Kojo, twenty-five years old, Kakogawa City, Hyogo Prefecture:

"I used to have rough skin, which I presume was caused by a weak stomach and intestinal tract, and I also got pimples frequently.

"From time to time, I took a digestive aid or juice of aloe, but because of its bitterness and bad smell I frequently stopped practicing that remedy. I began to take Green Barley Essence at the suggestion of my friend. I found it unexpectedly easy to drink. For three months, I have taken a large spoonful of Green Barley Essence two or three times a day. Now, the pimples have disappeared and the rough skin has become smooth and vivid. Moreover, my stomach has become healthy.

"When girls drink coffee in the office, I now usually drink fruit juice with Green Barley Essence in it."

Anemia

From Miss Kazuko Onishi, twenty-one years old, Nerima-ku, Tokyo:

"I used to suffer from anemia and sometimes felt dizzy whenever I got busy at work. I tried various hematonics, but was advised not to rely on drugs alone. I therefore began to take Green Barley Essence.

"I took Green Barley Essence dissolved in water when I awoke in the morning and before I went to bed. After two months, I noticed that I had no dizziness even when my work was busy. My complexion became better.

"I also feel that my tendency to get tired eyes has improved. I now regard Green Barley Essence as my doctor."

Sexual Life—Reduced Potency

From Mr. Isao Saita (pseudonym), thirty-five years old, Kawasaki City, Kanagawa Prefecture:

"After I turned thirty-five, I noticed I was becoming susceptible to fatigue and loss of vitality. I attributed this to my busy work and came to fear that I would not be able to live a normal life. Above all, I was concerned when I lost interest in my sexual life. I became impatient at the thought that I was too young to be in that condition. But the problem became worse as I grew more frustrated and tried to improve it.

"My wife then happened to suggest Green Barley Essence. I began to take it, not expecting much. Now, after six months, I am completely free from the fatigue I previously felt and have regained my vitality. I also have found my abdominal fatness subsiding a little and my sexual life returning to normal.

"I c   hankful for Green Barley
Esser   did not seriously believe it."

Cor

            .obuko Shimizu (pseudonym), age nine-
            .ura-ku, Kitakyushu:
            . am a nineteen-year-old student. From childhood, I
have been mentally unstable and have always felt
impatient. Many people say I lack good judgment. I
think that it is due to persistent constipation.

"When I entered college and began to live alone in
an apartment house, this trouble became even worse.
At one time, I was extremely uneasy about it. A pharmacist then suggested powdery Green Barley Essence. At
first, I doubted its effect and did not take much of it.
But, since my evacuation began to improve somewhat,
I have taken it every morning and night.

"Although constipation has not been completely cured,
I find myself more stable mentally and feel that I am
more quick in making decisions. My life has been
changed."

Shoulder Stiffness and Lumbago

From Mr. Zenji Matsuyama, fifty years old, Neyagawa,
Osaka:
"I am a bus driver. Probably because of tension during work, I had considerable shoulder stiffness which
was almost unbearable. I went to a professional massager.
The massager also practices ionization therapy and recommended Green Barley Essence, saying that massage
could relieve the stiffness but not cure it.

"Within a month after I began taking it, I found
myself without shoulder stiffness. When I had heavy

stiffness in my shoulders I was impatient during work, but now I enjoy my work very much."

Gastritis, Gastroptosis and Peptic Ulcer

From Mr. Masayuki Yokota, sixty years old, Oura, Nagasaki:

"I was diagnosed as having a peptic ulcer which was treated with an oral drug at a hospital at Nagasaki Medical College. I happened to hear the lecture of Dr. Hagiwara and consequently began to take Green Barley Essence. In about one month, I improved in appetite and gained about 4 kg (9 lbs). Later, one of the two ulcer sites was healed. I also felt no nausea which had troubled me every morning before I took Green Barley Essence. I believe my improved appetite led to the power of curing the disease from inside the body. I still keep taking Green Barley Essence earnestly."

Diabetes

From Mr. Shigeyuki Yamano, fifty-seven years old, Chigasaki, Kanagawa Prefecture:

"One year ago, I was diagnosed as having diabetes. I have succeeded in improving my constitution and curing the disease by taking only natural foods and green juices without any synthetic drugs.

"Before this cure, I could not do any work which required incessant attention. Now I can work energetically and my complexion has improved.

"What I took for this purpose included not only Green Barley Essence but also ordinary green juices, *hachimigan* (a Chinese herb drug), royal jelly, an enzyme preparation, honey, apple vinegar and a mushroom extract preparation. I cannot say for sure which of these was actually effective.

"In any case, I believe that it is best to cure diabetes by taking a carefully controlled diet and natural health-promoting foods which can improve the constitution."

Hypotension and Hypertension

From Mrs. Nobuko Matsui, thirty-three years old, Saseho City, Nagasaki Prefecture:

"After the birth of my third child, I developed hypertension. It caused me headaches and swelling in my left hand. I was compelled to lie in bed for three months after delivery.

"I continued to take the drug given by my physician, but at the same time I began to take Green Barley Essence at the suggestion of a sister of my husband. In about one month the headaches went away. The blood pressure did not easily decrease. But, at the end of five months, it dropped from 230/130 to 160/100.

"Furthermore, occasional bleeding from the nostrils stopped. Although I thought that my life might end at the age of thirty-three, I now see that my life has been saved."

Heart Disease

From Mr. Yuji Koga, fifty years old, Beppu City, Oita Prefecture:

"My wife, who has been weak all her life, finally collapsed not long ago. After a detailed examination, she was diagnosed as having a fairly serious case of valvular heart disease.

"She was hospitalized at once but the doctor said that because of her age she didn't have the strength to withstand an operation. The doctor told me that it was important for her to eat alkaline foods. I therefore attempted to have her take Green Barley Essence at the suggestion of my friend.

"At first I feared whether my wife, who is of a neurotic nature, would take it. However, she found it tasty and began to drink a glass of Green Barley Essence in water every morning and night. I myself began to take it. She has stopped having frequent dizziness resulting from high blood pressure, and she seems to have changed in character.

"Since she began to take Green Barley Essence she has had a good appetite and a good complexion. At first I gave up the hope of her recovery. But now she will be able to leave the hospital soon."

Nephrosis

From Mrs. Masae Yamamura, thirty-five years old, Hitoyoshi City, Kumamoto Prefecture:

"My eldest son, now in the fourth grade of primary school, was diagnosed as having nephrosis at an early age. He has been hospitalized many times. When he was in the hospital his condition improved a little but he always regressed to his original condition in about three months. He had to be absent from school so often that he could not catch up with the other children.

"Finally, I was informed of the existence of Green Barley Essence by a person who said it cured his renal disease. Like a drowning person who catches at a straw, I began to let my son take Green Barley Essence. After leaving the hospital, he continued to take it for one year. I have tried to reduce animal protein in his diet and replace it with as much vegetable protein as possible. After several months of this, I noticed that his urine became clearer and flowed better. Furthermore, the edema that had appeared whenever he got tired and the cloudiness in his eyes disappeared. Thus, for a year, he has had no need to be hospitalized. Although his condition has not been completely cured, he goes to school every day.

"I now believe that it is good diet and Green Barley Essence which will save my son, not drugs."

Cirrhosis Hepatitis

From Zennosuke Yamaguchi, forty-one years old, Sumiyoshi-ku, Osaka:

"I run a small company. Probably because I over-worked myself or drank too much in entertaining customers, I came down with liver trouble and was hospitalized for about three months. When I was permitted to leave the hospital, I again had to work hard. A blood examination soon showed that the disease was worse.

"Feeling hopeless, I began to think I would have to choose whether to destroy the company or my health. At the suggestion of a business friend, I began to take Green Barley Essence. At first I doubted its effectiveness. But with a certain amount of desperation, I drank about five glasses of Green Barley Essence every day. In two months my disease was completely cured.

"Neither the doctor nor I could believe it. But repeated examinations have revealed no illness. It was like a miracle.

"Now, my business goes well and so does my health. Green Barley Essence is to thank."

Inhibition of Cancer

From Mr. Junji Ishiyama, fifty-eight years old, Nakabe, Kanagawa Prefecture:

"I was diagnosed as having gastric cancer in an early stage. For six months, I ate a special diet consisting mainly of unpolished rice and vegetables. At the same time, I was given a Suzuki-type visible ray therapy. About one month ago, I also began to practice loquat-leaf therapy. At that time, Dr. Suzuki recommended Green Barley Essence. The cancer vanished at the end of six months after I began the visible ray therapy. My persistent constipation also disappeared. I have found my stomach and intestines in good condition and feel very comfortable.

"I feel lighter in the legs and seem to be more healthy than before."

GREEN BARLEY ESSENCE STIMULATES THE HEALTH WITHIN

In this short selection of letters we have been told that Green Barley Essence is as effective against obesity and skin blemishes as it is against heart disease and cancer. How can this be? Does it sound as if I have found a miracle drug? That is not what I am suggesting. Green Barley Essence should never be used as a cure-all any more than it should be used as a treatment for any particular disease. Curative claims for drugs and preparations have met with suspicion and rejection through the centuries, and rightly so.

What should be regarded as the cure-all is the human body itself. It is we ourselves who effect the cure of our diseased bodies by the right application of nutrients and by the formation of healthful attitudes that lead us away from habits that bring ruin from within. I believe that the apparent effectiveness of Green Barley Essence as shown in these letters is, above all, proof of how far we have strayed from the natural course of health.

What Manages Life Activities?

As I have said, the direct incentive which drove me to an earnest study of green juices, particularly those of barley leaves, was the study of Chinese medicine.

I recognized the effects of these medicinal herbs which mankind cultivated from its long experience. There are countless cases in which Chinese herb medicines helped restore the ill to good health. I believe this was accomplished by reviving the normal functioning of organs that got out of order. There is no doubt the herbs work well on certain symptoms. But, what is the essence of medicinal herbs? I hoped to ascertain which of the many ingredients in them work to cure a particular disease and how.

Though my research was successful commercially, I cannot say I have learned which of the many medicinal herbs in a certain Chinese drug are effective against a specific disease. That determination would have required a systematic research project comprising the efforts of many researchers, while I was working alone in a laboratory.

Yet, finally, I came to a very simple realization—that the fundamental method of Chinese medicines is to restore man's distorted physiological functions to their normal condition. In other words, the mechanism of controlling life activities within the body can be restored from a diseased to a healthy condition beginning with life's building blocks. The truth is that much attention is placed upon disease, as if disease were a tangible thing. In reality, it is merely the absence of health, the defeat of the life force in a part of the living body.

Often this loss of health originates on a mental and emotional level before showing up as a physical disease. Acupuncture provides one example of the ability to restore a normal pattern to the body's activities by influencing its energy. The thrust of Chinese herbal medicine is similar to this in that it restores the natural flow of energies in the body rather than working against the disease.

This, however, is tantamount to the mere conclusion that Chinese herb drugs are effective. To go a step further than that becomes difficult, and I must resort to an analysis which is partly scientific and partly metaphysical.

Building Blocks for the Growth of Cells

There are many paradoxes in the study of human health. Many of you might doubt that every human being carries the tubercle bacillus. This is true, however, but most people are not infected by tuberculosis. While having various viruses in the body, some people become ill, but others do not. In other words, some people have great resistance to viruses, while others have weak resistance whatever preventive measures they take.

The same can be said with regard to the problem of potency. There are men capable of fathering children at the age of seventy. Some women can become pregnant at the age of fifty. In some people various organs and tissues within the body are active and in others they are inactive. The same person, too, may be vigorous at one time but not at other times. What stimulates the living body and invigorates the activities of the organs? And what causes the differences among individuals?

Human cells have their own lifetimes. Skin cells and hair incessantly metabolize and are regenerated. But liver cells are slow to regenerate. Brain cells, on the other hand, grow to mature form before the age of three and remain unchanged during the lifespan of a person. Rather, as one grows old, the brain cells degenerate and decrease in number, leading to cerebromalacia.

There is something in the tissues of a human being which stimulates and invigorates the body into performing life activities. This is considered the cause for the differences between individuals. I found this during the course of my investigations into the components of the young leaves of barley. My research team and I succeeded in extracting this active component from the green juices of young barley leaves.

The presence of this ingredient in Green Barley Essence may prove useful to research being conducted in the new field of biotechnology. It involves creating a special cell and growing it industrially in large quantities. Experiments have shown that when the cultivation is carried out in the presence of Green Barley Essence, cell growth becomes strikingly vigorous. Consequently, it has been reasoned that Green Barley Essence has the action of invigorating and promoting cell growth. Further investigations led to the discovery that a low-molecular weight, water-soluble protein in Green Barley Essence cures ulcers, and promotes new growth of cells and formation of surface skin and mucous membranes.

The young leaves of barley contain components which act like a growth hormone. Tryptophan, a kind of amino acid, is one such component. It is well-known that tryptophan is outstandingly effective for the treatment of dwarfism because abnormally undersized persons lack an enzyme which produces tryptophan.

Thus it can be seen that Green Barley Essence contains an abundance of substances which invigorate the living body and promote its growth.

In the next chapter I will take a more detailed look at each of the examples presented in the previous letters to show how some of the individual ingredients in Green Barley Essence work to create this invigorating, cell-growth promoting action within the body to help restore health as the normal state of being.

First, I will cover general health topics such as complexion, obesity and anemia; then I will examine some more serious conditions on which Green Barley Essence appears to have pharmacological effects.

CHAPTER 7 ▭▭▭▭▭▭▭▭▭▭▭▭▭▭▭

DIET FOR GOOD HEALTH

THE NUTRIENT HEALING PROCESS

NATURAL AGING of the skin leads to roughness, pigment deposition, pimples and other eruptions. It weakens the resistance of all membranes, leading to inflammation by even the slightest stimulation. The weakening of the skin represents a weakening of the internal organs.

Conversely, we can say that when the internal organs grow weak, so does the skin. Trouble in the stomach and intestines causes rough skin and eruptions. This will show first in membranes of the eyes or lips. Persons with cloudy eyes or a swollen face can also be afflicted in the liver or kidneys. It is for this reason that physicians first examine the complexion, the luster of the skin, and the mucous membrane when making a diagnosis.

And, for the same reason, I will begin my discussion of health topics with the skin, our barometer of health.

The Skin as a Reflecting Mirror

Skin and beauty. They seem inseparable. Unfortu-· nately, so dependent is the beauty of a face upon the appearance of the skin that young women today will pile their faces with makeup in the hope of attaining beauty, even at the age when they have the fairest skin. I think women should pay closer attention to the health of the skin by giving it the best possible nutrition.

Creams and skin drugs for external application may sometimes be helpful, but what is primarily required is a food which is called "a high-grade drug" in Chinese medicine.

According to Chinese medicine, drugs are classified into high-, medium- and low-grade drugs. The low-grade drugs are toxicants. The medium-grade drugs work either as toxicants or curing agents. The high-grade drugs are natural foods which bring the functions of the internal organs to a normal state.

This means that what is required is only a food which contains abundant minerals, enzymes and vitamins which will rejuvenate the cells of the internal organs and of the skin. Raw vegetables, especially green vegetables, are best for this purpose.

As one of the highest foods in this spectrum, Green Barley Essence will rejuvenate the skin through this direct connection with the internal organs. As regards minerals, seaweeds are also an important source.

This might be the reason why it is said that the skin of Japanese women is very beautiful. Seaweeds are not included in the typical diet in such places as America and Russia. This fact is probably related to the fact that the skin of women in these countries is susceptible to chapping, freckles and pigment deposition.

Medically, the phenomenon I have been describing is referred to as the Brown-Sequard law of cutaneovisceral reflex. The idea of the skin "mimicking" the internal organs may seem somewhat strange, but we often experience it in daily life when we sip warm coffee and immediately feel the whole body become warm. This is not because the hot coffee is absorbed from the stomach and raises the body temperature. In fact, when hot coffee comes into the stomach, the blood vessels in the mucous membrane of the stomach dilate, as do the capillary blood vessels of the skin, making the body feel warm. For the same reason, when we drink ice water in summer, we feel cool. When cold water comes into the stomach, the blood vessels of the stomach shrink, and the capillary blood vessels on the surface of the skin shrink. That is why we feel cool after drinking cold water. This is the effect of Brown-Sequard's law, which I have found through my own study to be highly relevant to the rejuvenation of the skin.

As a matter of fact, I have been studying the subject of skin rejuvenation for a long time. This endeavor began in 1956, when I was introduced by Professor Shinzo Hayami of Kansai Medical College to Professor Tadayoshi Arakawa of the dermatology section of Tokushima University. At that time, I was thinking of trying gastrointestinal drugs for the rejuvenation of the skin. I made this suggestion to Professor Arakawa, who completely agreed with my idea and emphasized the significance of Brown-Sequard's law.

World-Famous Hair-Nourishing Agent

I first selected *Swertia japonica*, a medicinal herb which has been used in Japan as a folk remedy for gastric and intestinal troubles. I started with the simple expectation that it would improve the secretion of the digestive fluid, thereby ensuring healthy stomach and intestines which, in turn, would invigorate the skin.

In the course of repeated experiments, I found an interesting thing. Ingestion of *Swertia japonica* resulted in the dilation of the capillary vessels of the skin, thus leading to increased blood flow into the hair roots. Accordingly, nutrients reached the hair sufficiently to sustain good growth.

I am not a pathologist but a pharmacist. So I could not be content with the results of my research unless I could find a practical application for it. I immediately set to work looking for one.

Out of this study emerged a hair-nourishing agent sold under the trade name Shiden. Its introduction was extensively reported in the press, including the *New York Times*. Professor Arakawa and I were invited to Munich University, Cambridge University, the University of Chicago and the University of California to explain it.

In Japan, Professor Arakawa organized the Dermatologic Function Research Center at Tokushima University. I continued my study there for some time, becoming increasingly confident in the saying that "the skin is a reflecting mirror of the internal organs." I believe that the functions of the internal organs cannot be neglected in the treatment of skin diseases and efforts to rejuvenate the skin.

The effective activities of Green Barley Essence on the rejuvenation of the skin were demonstrated by clinical experiments on patients with skin diseases conducted by Dr. Tatsuo Muto, a dermatologist in Kurume, a city in southern Japan. These experiments were made public in a meeting of a professional society under the title "Curing of Skin Diseases by a Green Juice Extract of the Young Leaves of Barley," as reported in the *Nippon Keizai* newspaper on June 7, 1975.

The report said that the symptoms were improved in

a fifty-seven-year-old patient with melanosis and a sixteen-year-old victim of atopic dermatitis after taking Green Barley Essence for more than five months. Of twenty-five dermatologic patients tested, those who took Green Barley Essence recovered earlier than those who did not; at the same time, improvement of blood flow, bowel movement, appetite and recovery from fatigue were observed.

Retards Aging of Cells

Earlier I noted that my research efforts succeeded in isolating the agent in Green Barley Essence which slows the aging of cells. This agent is the enzyme superoxide dismutase (SOD), which was discovered from the blood of a cow some years ago by a professor at the University of California. Before that, a British scientist pointed out that erythrocytes, or red blood cells, of the human blood contain a relatively large amount of a special protein. This protein has now turned out to be SOD.

As I shall show later, SOD is an extremely important enzyme now receiving attention in the treatment of cancer. For the moment, I will briefly mention how SOD helps rejuvenate the cells. In the course of respiration and metabolism, hazardous active forms of oxygen are constantly being expelled. One is the superoxide radical (O_2^-). This radical has a very strong oxidizing power capable of decomposing cells. Fortunately, however, the enzyme SOD works within a living organism to destroy the active oxygens.

Recent investigations have shown that the internal organs in relatively long-living primates contain a large quantity of this enzyme within the cells. It has therefore been assumed that SOD will prevent aging of cells of our body, and has to do with longevity.

As the role of enzymes has been increasingly understood, SOD has enjoyed a vogue among health food enthusiasts in the United States. Most of the commercially available SOD is extracted from the liver of cattle. As the liver is the detoxifying organ, and as many cattle are injected with steroids to build muscle tissue, this product is of questionable value. On the other hand, Green Barley Essence has one of the highest natural SOD levels of any plant, making it superior as a source of this vital enzyme.

The action of enzymes in Green Barley Essence is also effective against pigment deposition, melanosis and pimples. The best way to understand how this happens is to first examine why these symptoms occur.

Pigment deposition results from the oxidation of tyrosine, an amino acid, by an enzyme called tyrosinase. The tyrosine changes to melanin, a dark pigment, which is deposited in the skin.

Here again, the enzyme system plays an important role. If the enzymes within the living body are working normally, oxidation of tyrosine does not occur. Even if it does occur, the deposited melanin is removed, since the skin is always performing vigorous metabolism.

If pigment deposition caused by some stimulation disappears rapidly, there is no skin problem apparent. Long-term deposition is due, presumably, to an imbalance of enzymes. Ingestion of Green Barley Essence will help prevent this by helping to keep the enzymes in balance.

Melanin is also involved in the process of sunburning. Until recently. sunburn had been considered to be an inflammation of the skin by ultraviolet rays. But it has been found that a more complex interaction within the cells is involved.

When sunlight strikes the skin directly, the energy

metabolism of the cells becomes exceedingly vigorous as the cells are excited by solar energy. This causes the cellular fluids to release magnesium, calcium and potassium, and permits the inflow of a sodium ion.

Since this is the case, I suppose sunburn could be inhibited by taking Green Barley Essence either before or after sunbathing. Since there are no experimental data or clinical cases, this is, of course, my own postulation.

Helps Overweight

As far as overweight is concerned, it is not merely a matter of one's appearance but is likely to lead to high blood pressure, heart disease and arteriosclerosis. In particular, overweight in middle-aged and old persons almost always leads to these diseases.

As we know, this has become the age of "high-calorie" nutrition. Our diets contain oil and fat, polished rice, white bread and white refined sugar in quantities which make them difficult to fully burn within the body. Burning is a process which finally renders caloric food into water and carbon dioxide gas which is expelled from the body. If complete burning fails, these materials remain undecomposed and are stored as fat under the skin or in fat cells.

The burning process, called lipid metabolism, is aided by cytochrome oxidase, an enzyme found in the mitochondria of "brown cells" (a type of fat cell) within the body. Minerals and vitamins are very important in promoting lipid metabolism and the action of mitochondria.

The usual remedy for weight loss is a diet therapy which consists of eating foods low in caloric value. It is based on minimizing sugars, starch, and fats which tend to build up as subcutaneous fats. These foods are replaced by vegetable fats which include, for example, sesame oil, olive oil, safflower oil, and colza oil and margarine made from such oils. They contain unsaturated fatty acids which can dissolve cholesterol deposited on the vascular walls. However, vegetable fats are still foods of high caloric value.

The best method of weight control, I believe, is to promote the action of enzymes which activate the brown cells and aid in lipid metabolism. As I have shown, Green Barley Essence is rich in these enzymes. For this reason, I consider the active components of juices from the young leaves of barley a far better alternative to weight control than the typical approach of dieting.

Anyway, it is unhealthy to abstain from meals or take only water to achieve weight loss. And unwise. Once the practitioner of this method resumes eating as usual, he or she will again become overweight.

The problem of overweight is inseparable from the metabolism of the thyroid hormone. When there is too much fat, its metabolism is promoted by this hormone. If the secretion of the thyroid hormone decreases, weight gain will result.

Once, thyroid hormone preparations were used extensively as weight control drugs in the belief that the administration of thyroid hormone would remove overweight. However, thyroid hormones were found to retard the function of the thyroid gland with long-term use. This is the same as the relation of adrenocortical hormone preparations to the adrenal gland, mentioned earlier. Even a case of mental disorder was reported as a consequence of administering this hormone. This soon led the U.S. Food and Drug Administration to prohibit the use of thyroid hormone preparations, except when prescribed by a physician.

Green Barley Essence is not a special drug against obesity, and there is no guarantee that taking it will immediately lead to weight reduction. In order to get rid of excess weight, it is first of all necessary to improve your diet. Abstain from fats, starch and sugars as much as possible and engage in moderate physical exercise. If, in addition to this, you take one teaspoonful of Green Barley Essence three times a day, you will soon find yourself losing weight. For Green Barley Essence, the most alkaline of foods, neutralizes the acidity of the body fluids and spontaneously invigorates the function of the thyroid gland. It would be ideal to take seaweeds, a source of iodine required for the production of thyroid hormones, in addition to Green Barley Essence.

Furthermore, the activities of a number of enzymes contained in Green Barley Essence can also be expected. For example, lipase, an enzyme which decomposes fats deposited within the body, is also contained in Green Barley Essence. Moreover, many enzymes which normalize the various functions within the body are directly absorbed from the intestinal tract, and act immediately. If the functions which our body inherently possesses work vigorously, there should be no abnormal weight.

That "Fruits Can Help Weight Loss" Is a Myth

Incidentally, we must be very careful about fructose (or fruit sugars) and fruits, which are used extensively as a food of low caloric value. We often see girls who want to lose weight eat only fruits for lunch. But their goal will not be achieved, as it has recently been demonstrated that fructose changes to fat within the body more rapidly than common sugar and starch. The fructose in pineapples and bananas changes to fat as soon as it comes into the body. Fruits are regarded as alkaline foods because they contain abundant minerals, but their content of substances changeable to fat is far larger than their mineral content, so that the effects of minerals are almost negligible.

Use in Fasting Cure

Fasting cure, or abstention from meals, is frequently practiced as a remedy for overweight. This results in a loss of weight because organic matters, including fats which are deposited within the body, are burned rapidly. This apparently removes overweight. But sometimes, after fasting, one may become bloated from water. This is because when eating is resumed, moisture in the food is entirely absorbed, causing swelling of the cells. Fasting is an effective method, but for the restoration of the vigor to the body, it is necessary to eat foods having an abundance of proteins, minerals and vitamins. For this purpose, Green Barley Essence, containing these ingredients in a well-balanced state, is the best choice. It can restore cells tired from food abstention to a vigorous state.

You may take Green Barley Essence during a fast. Even while fasting, the body keeps metabolizing and a supply of minerals is essential. If you get your minerals from Green Barley Essence, you will be able to avoid many risks which are associated with the fasting cure.

Effective Against Constipation

In mentioning digestive activities, we should not forget constipation, which is often taken lightly, but should not be. It is rightly said that good eating, good sleeping and good evacuation are the three barometers of health. These factors, if disordered, cause disease.

Prolonged constipation causes a swelling or pressing feeling in the abdomen, and this naturally leads to a loss of appetite. Furthermore, since it also causes head-ache or dizziness, the problem inhibits good sleep. It is no wonder that as a result, its victim becomes suscepti-ble to fatigue and mental instability.

In such a case, Green Barley Essence dissolved in water is absolutely effective. The active ingredients in Green Barley Essence promote the mobility of the intesti-nal tract, and also strengthen the muscles required for evacuation.

Habitual constipation, which is frequently found in persons over about forty, is due mainly to the reduced mobility of the large intestines and the reduced muscu-lar power of the entire body. As we have seen in Chapter 5, the potassium contained in Green Barley Essence effectively counters loss of intestinal function and reduced muscular power.

Usually, people say that vegetables are effective against constipation. However, to those whose stomach and intestines have reduced functions or to the elderly, the fibrous tissues of vegetables become a burden because of their resistance to digestion. Since Green Barley Essence is free of fibrous tissues, these people can take it without anxiety.

A Storage House of Blood

Another problem related to diet is anemia. I have heard of a new affliction which frequently strikes office workers in high rise, air-conditioned office buildings. Its symptom is sudden numbness in the legs and it can be severe enough to require hospitalization. This is not un-common among the aged, but today many young women are being stricken. Many are found to suffer anemia.

Statistics on nutrition compiled by Japan's Ministry of Welfare and Health show that anemia has become widespread. About one-fourth of all women have anemia or a tendency toward it. Although the number of anemic patients is relatively small in younger males, the number is larger in males in their fifties than in females. Recently, anemia has also increased in high school boys. It sometimes goes unnoticed because its symptoms are confused with those of overexertion.

Why has anemia increased despite the fact that the amount of animal proteins ingested has shown such a great increase? The great number of cases of anemia among the Japanese is due probably to an imbalance of nutrition.

Production of blood requires an iron ion, a copper ion and a potassium ion, as well as protein. Without these mineral ions, hemoglobin would be difficult to form. In addition, a vitamin, folic acid, is also essential for blood formation.

Even those foods which are naturally high in vitamins do little good when consumed in processed form. Vitamins are destroyed during processing. The iron component changes under heat to iron oxide, not easily absorbed by the body.

As a curing treatment for anemia, an iron preparation containing reduced iron has previously been used. This is not sufficient for blood formation. Since Green Barley Essence contains iron in the organically bonded state, or as divalent iron, it can be immediately absorbed from the intestinal tract. The abundance of protein and minerals in Green Barley Essence has been repeatedly mentioned in this book. Green Barley Essence can be said to be a storage house of blood.

Wonderful Deodorizing Activity of Chlorophyll

Bad smells such as body odor and foul breath are problems that cannot be made light of. How unfortunate when a kiss which must connect two lovers closely becomes the cause of a decisive parting.

Such an unfortunate accident can be avoided if the lovers drink or gargle a glass of Green Barley Essence dissolved in water before dating. In this case, unlike our previous examples of abnormal constitution or other disease, the effect of Green Barley Essence is immediate. This fast-acting effect is due to the chlorophyll contained in Green Barley Essence. Scientists universally recognize that chlorophyll has a rapid deodorizing activity.

Medicine of Chlorophyll, a book published by the Association of Life Science, reports the following experimental results obtained by Dr. Keichi Morishita and Dr. Kaneo Hotta on a panel of people subjected to various known causes of foul breath:

1) Chlorophyll removed the odor of garlic in 70 percent to 80 percent of those tested within 10 to 20 minutes.
2) Chlorophyll removed breath traces of various wines and liquors within 30 minutes in 80 percent of the panel.
3) Chlorophyll removed breath odors in 80 percent of a panel suffering gastric trouble within 30 minutes.
4) Chorophyll removed the odor of cigarettes from a panel of smokers within 10 to 30 minutes.

These results followed ingestion of 3 to 12 grams of chlorophyll. The report concludes that greater effects would be expected if larger doses were used.

Anti-inflammatory Activity Increases Its Deodorizing Activity

In addition to its direct deodorizing activity, chlorophyll possesses anti-inflammatory and germicidal activities, as mentioned in detail in Chapter 4. These activities sometimes contribute to the alleviation of alveolar blennorrhea and inflammation in the oral cavity which cause foul odors.

Offensive odors emitting from vaginal discharge are of concern to women. Deodorizing activity and a bit of germicidal and anti-inflammatory activities make Green Barley Essence effective against this problem. Direct application in a vaginal cleaning solution will be more effective than the use of it as an internal drug.

At one time it was believed that body odors resulted from the secretion of a bad-smelling fluid from the apocrine gland situated mainly in the armpit and the pubic region. I have found this to be erroneous for the following reason.

I found that the fluids secreted from the apocrine gland do not have a bad smell, but that the secreted substances are decomposed by bacteria to cause the smell. I came to this conclusion after I applied an agent having a strong germicidal activity to the armpit of a person who suffered from body odor, and the odor almost disappeared. If a fluid originally having a bad smell were secreted from the body, the smell wouldn't disappear upon application of a germicide.

From this experience, I believe the chlorophyll contained in Green Barley Essence acts dually against body odor. On one hand, it exerts an indirect deodorizing activity, and on the other, it kills germs and removes the very cause of body odor.

Physical Strength and Health Are the Basis of Potency

Sexual freedom exists today in Japan to a greater extent than in any past age. Abundant information about sexual life is prevalent. But not a few young men complain of reduced potency, and sometimes impotence. The dissatisfaction is only augmented by the prevailing information about sex. There have been an increasing number of cases where this finally led to divorce.

Green Barley Essence can help increase potency. Today, the many "sex consultants" who give advice on this subject commonly cite physical strength and health as the basis for improving sexual power. Needless to say, Green Barley Essence is effective for this most important factor.

Increases the Potency of Sperm

Green Barley Essence contains abundant isoflavone. Since isoflavone is regarded as a kind of estrogenic substance, it is not surprising that some people claim that Green Barley Essence imparts vitality and increases the secretion of seminal fluid. It also has a tendency to enlarge the breasts and promote the secretion of milk.

I have recently started experiments on the relation between Green Barley Essence and sex hormones in mice. Under a microscope I examined the testicles of mice which were given a water solution of Green Barley Essence and others which were simply given water. It appeared that the number of sperm was greater in the mice given Green Barley Essence. I look forward to experimental data which will clearly show the ability of Green Barley Essence to increase sexual energy.

The problem of potassium and magnesium ions is also

involved in this matter. Sexual intercourse is performed not only by the shrinking motion of the vaginal muscle of the female but also by the partial muscular shrinking motion of the male. By this muscular motion, potassium in the cells is excreted, and a sodium ion is taken in. This is quite the same as muscular motions in general. In other words, the cells become short of ions such as potassium or calcium ions. If this condition lasts, the muscles required for sexual intercourse do not work adequately, and no satisfaction can be obtained.

Removes Mental Stress and Promotes Circulation

Back and shoulder stiffness and lumbago are perennial nuisances which seem to be increasing nowadays. Probably this is why sauna houses are now enjoying great popularity.

These troubles come mainly from mental stress and an excessive intake of acidic foods. When we eat acidic foods, acidic substances such as lactic acid are prone to accumulate within the body. These substances combine with proteins in the muscles to form lactic acid proteins which build up in the tissues. If this cycle is repeated, heavy shoulder stiffness and lumbago and also gout result.

Those who suffer from these painful ailments should engage in moderate physical exercise such as walking or playing golf and increase their consumption of raw vegetables having a high degree of alkalinity to enhance the metabolism in the body. This lightens and refreshes the body, consequently improving circulation. The natural remedy of relaxation will only be successful if done in conjunction with a low-acid diet.

Asthma and Allergy Can Be Improved by Diet

In the industrial districts of Kawasaki, Yokkaichi, Keiyo and Kitakyushu, Japan, there has been found to be a an unnaturally high percentage of persons suffering from infantile asthma and other allergic diseases. This fact is, of course, a serious problem. But we cannot afford to simply point an accusing finger at smoke and waste gases from factories and forget how feeble we have allowed our bodies to become through insufficient nutrition.

If given a chance, the human body can do a pretty good job of defending itself, as the following experiment demonstrates. When we remove the lid of a sterilized Petri dish, then close it after a lapse of several seconds and allow it to stand at 98.6° F., a very large number of bacteria are seen to grow in it. Where do they come from? From the innumerable number of pathogenic bacteria and fungi always present in the air.

There are various pathogenic bacteria and fungi adhering at all times to the fingertips or the mucous membrane of the skin, but we still do not always get a disease. Even when infected by bacteria, some people get sick and others do not.

The same relation exists between air pollution and allergic patients. If a person of an allergic constitution lives in polluted air, he naturally will undergo a different reaction than a healthy person. Furthermore, persons who are quite healthy in clean air may have a different reaction in polluted air, but still not show such a reaction in the form of disease. In view of this, it is most important to make the body strong so it can withstand a bad environment. The tough body, in which normal cells are working actively, is made possible only by daily diet.

Adrenocortical Hormones Only Make Diseases Chronic

Allergic problems tend to be chronic and difficult to cure by traditional medicine. These include urticaria, bronchial asthma including infantile asthma, chronic eczema typified by atopic dermatitis, acute eczema, rhinitis and rheumatism.

It is believed that allergic diseases are associated with immunoreactions within the body, but their causes have not yet been completely elucidated. For this reason, no decisive therapeutic method has been available.

An examination of patients with allergies shows that their blood pH is on the acidic side, while it should normally be alkaline.

Adrenocortical hormones (steroids) have been frequently used for allergic diseases to stop itching and pain or as anti-inflammatory agents. They did not fundamentally cure the diseases, but there were dramatic effects on inflammation. These hormones were abused, and caused considerable side effects. The omnipresent abuse of these hormones finally led the United Nations to issue a notification recommending that these adrenocortical hormone preparations not be used as internal drugs.

Frequently, allergic patients have a poor secretion of adrenocortical hormone. In healthy persons, the body reacts against external stimulation and can suppress symptoms that result from the stimulation. However, this function is not performed sufficiently in the allergic patient, and hence, therapy has been practiced to supply adrenocortical hormone agents from outside.

The problem with this therapy is that hormone-releasing organs, as I stated earlier, characteristically slow down their own production as soon as particular hormones are introduced from outside. If an adrenocortical hormone agent is used for a particular hormone-releasing organ which is out of order, the organ becomes more out of order. This is like giving money, apparel, and luxurious meals to lazy persons who won't work.

If we rub our skin hard, it becomes reddish. If one has an allergic constitution, even slight rubbing makes the skin reddish. It is due to dilation of the capillary vessels that the rubbed portion gets reddish or itchy. Rubbing the skin activates certain enzymes which then decompose proteins to form a histamine-like substance. The substance dilates the vessels in a way that causes liquid components of the blood to ooze from the vessels and induces itching. By this process, stimulation to the skin results in reddish swelling and itching.

If the skin becomes abnormal in this way, another enzyme such as histaminase comes into action to restore it to its normal condition. If the action of the histaminase is weak, however, even a slight stimulation results in an abnormal reaction in the skin.

Supplying Minerals Is a True Therapeutic Method Against Allergic Problems

Persons with allergic rhinitis or asthma are susceptible to colds, and in extreme cases, they have recurring colds year-round. Usually, aspirin, various pyrazolone derivatives and antihistamines are used to treat the colds. These drugs, when taken internally, cause acidification of the blood. The reaction is more pronounced when the preparation is injected, although it is not clear why. But there is every reason to believe that the following occurs:

When foreign matter (a substance which is absent in the body and does not participate in its physiological functions) is taken into the body, a reaction to remove it naturally goes into effect. This activity is that of cells and involves enzymes. At this time, the metabolization of minerals is considered to be temporarily increased. This leads to a temporary insufficiency of minerals within the body, which in turn is believed to cause acidification of body fluids.

If this is the case, then the hormone therapy in use today is like giving money voluntarily to a robber.

The important thing in treating allergic diseases is to make the adrenal glands and other internal organs return to normal metabolism.

For this purpose, it is absolutely necessary to maintain the ion balance of minerals within the cells so that a complex enzyme system may work sufficiently. The first thing that should be done is to improve the weakened fluids to a normal condition. The fundamental method of preventing allergic diseases would be to follow a diet high in alkaline foods, of which Green Barley Essence is the most effective. This preventive and curative method does not involve the risk of side effects.

Shortsightedness (Myopia) and Decayed Teeth

The striking increase in recent years of persons with shortsightedness and decayed teeth seems to me to be closely connected to mineral deficiency.

Some assert that the increased shortsightedness in children is due to excessive television viewing. Certainly, this is probably a part of the cause. But, if they stop watching television, will the number of the shortsighted decrease? I do not think so. Among the shortsighted, the constitution itself bears a propensity to shortsightedness, and this fact should be considered seriously.

In view of the mineral deficiency in our diet, it is

fully understandable that a deficiency in minerals, such as calcium in the retina or sclera (the anterior membrane of the eyeball), results in relaxation which in turn leads to shortsightedness.

The increase in tooth decay is induced also by a deficiency in calcium and other minerals. Decayed teeth are caused by the brittleness of a lime component which forms the teeth. It is calcium and other minerals which make up the lime component.

An excessive ingestion of sugars is another cause of decayed teeth. But we frequently see cases where a child who limits his intake of sweets and never fails to brush his teeth after ingestion has more decayed teeth than a child who eats as many sweets as he desires. Unfortunately, the mother who is making such an effort has probably forgotten one important thing—raw green vegetables. However hard she may try to exclude harmful substances, it gets her nowhere unless she makes an equal effort to improve her child's constitution.

The child who does not get decayed teeth even when he eats sweets probably ate green vegetables and therefore built up a strong constitution which rejected harmful substances.

Such a constitution is already built up in the fetal period. The constitution of the mother is directly transmitted to her child. Probably not only children with decayed teeth or shortsightedness, but also their mothers, dislike green vegetables, and thus are short of minerals.

Pregnant Women

It has long been known that the nutritive condition of the mother will affect the constitution, intelligence and nature of the child-to-be. The mother should therefore be very careful about her nutrition during pregnancy. It is questionable whether such care or efforts are being implemented adequately.

A woman cannot bear strong and healthy children if she follows a diet full of fats or processed instant foods. Moreover, when she eats foods containing harmful additives, these will affect her fetus, and may sometimes lead to abortion. In other cases, children are born with congenital microcephalus, malformation and insufficient growth.

If a woman does not take in enough alkaline foods, but eats only acidic food products, she will bear children with weak constitutions and impatient natures. There may be persons who won't believe this and will consider it absurd. But according to the research report of Drs. John Dobbing and Jean Sun of Manchester Medical College, Britain, the growth of nerve cells in the human brain begins at ten weeks after conception and ends at twenty weeks. Their report made it clear that undernourished infants become hypersensitive and impatient, and may sometimes exhibit motor abnormality.

A lady, an acquaintance of mine, has two children. The older one hardly eats vegetables but likes meat very much. He is weak, and has allergic asthma of a chronic nature. He is also susceptible to colds and has decayed teeth. She has more interest and knowledge about health than the ordinary person, and takes considerable care in bringing up her children. Despite this, the elder child is in poor health.

The younger child, who is just about three years younger, has a strong constitution and is quite healthy. He has good teeth, and only catches cold once in a very long while. His character is positive and cheerful. He also likes to eat vegetables.

The great difference, she told me, was her diet during pregnancy. One year before the birth of her second child she reconsidered her diet and took abundant vegetables in her diet.

"There may be another factor, but I believe this is the most decisive one. I can't think of any other reasonable cause. I think it strange, and at the same time feel rather horrible to see such a great difference between the two children," said the mother.

This, however, is not a strange thing, but is rather natural in view of the fact that the fetus grows as a result of receiving nutrients from its mother.

The same can be said with regard to barley, the raw material for Green Barley Essence. When the same seeds of barley are sown, there will be a difference in the component of the young leaves according to the soil and natural conditions. According to my experience, the mineral content decreases in barley grown on soil which is infertile and hardly contains minerals. Also, under poor conditions, the vitamin content decreases drastically.

The mother is "the soil" for the fetus, so it is clear how important the balance of nutrition is in pregnant women. For these reasons, I recommend Green Barley Essence in the diet of pregnant women.

PHARMACOLOGICAL EFFECTS OF
GREEN BARLEY ESSENCE

In the previous section, we saw how feeble we have allowed our bodies to become. Nutritional imbalance has led to obesity (overweight), chapped skin, anemia, myopia (shortsightedness), decayed teeth and other troubles which are not within the category of "disease." However, these troubles might lead to real diseases. Now, as never before, our condition demands prophylactic or preventive medicine. The preventive effect of

Green Barley Essence against these troubles has been fully stated.

Let us now see how its pharmacological effects can be exerted on actual diseases such as diabetes, hypertension, heart disease, peptic ulcer and pancreatitis.

Of course, Green Barley Essence is a natural health food and not a pharmaceutical. But, in fact, it has a curative effect on certain diseases and also, I am convinced, can inhibit cancerous cells.

Some people doubt that Green Barley Essence could have a noticeable effect on such diseases. I believe these doubts result from an overbelief in synthetic pharmaceuticals and a lack of understanding that we ourselves are the creators of disease as well as health.

My assertion of the surprising pharmacological effects of Green Barley Essence is based on the experiences of consumers and clinical data offered by physicians.

Even Infants Are Subject to Diabetes

Let us start with diabetes, a heartbreaking disease. There is no specific drug against diabetes.

At one time, synthetic drugs such as biguanides or sulfonylureas were frequently used to treat diabetes, but these drugs were soon prohibited because they were found to cause hepatic disorders. The only drug now being used for the treatment of diabetes is a synthetic hormonal preparation of insulin, filling in for the insulin that is normally secreted by the pancreas. Like adrenocortical hormones, it has a side effect of reducing the function of the pancreas when administered over a long period of time.

Diabetes is a disease caused by an abnormal decomposition of glycogen in the body due to a reduction of insulin. Glycogen is continuously decomposed to glucose which flows through the blood. If the amount of insulin decreases, the glycogen, which is usually stored in the liver and muscles as a source of energy, is decomposed to sugar. Thus, the patient becomes inactive and thin. The excess sugar within the blood is excreted out of the body in the form of urine and sweat.

The hormone called insulin serves to change the sugars within the body to glycogen in order to store it in the liver. According to the conventional concept, diabetes is caused by poor secretion of insulin. Recent studies, however, reveal that the blood of patients with juvenile diabetes contains more, not less, insulin. The question then comes up as to why the activity of insulin is weak in spite of its secretion in a larger amount.

Further investigations have shown that the glycogen-storing activity of insulin does not work well when the blood is acidic. Conversely, when the blood is alkaline, the activity of insulin becomes smooth. It has also been made clear that epinephrine, a hormone with the opposite effects of insulin, is secreted from the adrenal gland. When the blood becomes acidic, epinephrine greatly increases the sugar level in the blood, and when it becomes alkaline, the epinephrine loses its effect. Thus, when the blood becomes acidified, these two opposite hormones act synergistically to increase the blood sugar level, leading to diabetes. When the blood becomes alkaline, the blood sugar level is lowered, and the diabetes is improved.

In view of this, it is clear that a fundamental help for diabetes is to alkalinize the body. Since minerals maintain the alkalinity of body fluids, it is natural that Green Barley Essence, abundant in minerals, is effective against diabetes.

Diabetes patients not only have high blood sugar levels, but they can also develop complications such as hypertension caused by high cholesterol, blood vessel troubles, neuralgia, gastrointestinal troubles and impotence.

In order to prevent diabetes, it is necessary to maintain a healthy pancreas. Green Barley Essence exhibits a superior effect for this goal.

Cerebral Hemorrhage, Heart and Liver Troubles

When muscles are used for physical exercise or labor, potassium is excreted from the body fluids and sodium is built up. This principle is applicable to the way in which all our internal organs function.

This principle is applicable to the mobility of the intestinal tract; and the same can be said with regard to heart and liver troubles. Today, nearly 70 percent of the causes of mortality are cancer, cerebral hemorrhage, heart diseases and liver diseases.

Green Barley Essence is very effective in preventing these diseases. Let me use the example of heart disease to show why.

The value of high-potassium foods was suggested by a research report on hypertensive patients in a northeast district of Japan, noted for its high percentage of people with hypertension. In the report, a comparative study of hypertensive patients in Akita Prefecture and Aomori Prefecture, both in the above district, was given. The report said that the number of hypertensive patients in Akita Prefecture was much larger than that in Aomori Prefecture, and assigned the difference to the fact that more rice and salty pickles were eaten in Akita Prefecture, whereas in Aomori Prefecture, which is famous for apple production, people tended to eat more apples, which contain potassium.

The activity of the heart depends on enzymatic activity within the heart muscles. In order to keep the heart sound, potassium is indispensable. In a myocardial infarction, potassium is released from the cardiac muscles and the function of the heart ceases.

In the case of mental stress, the same phenomenon occurs in the body fluids. Under stress, the activities of our pituitary gland and adrenal cortex are spontaneously stimulated, and the secretion of adrenocortical hormone increases in order to alleviate the stress. At this time, a great change occurs in the metabolic system for sodium and potassium, leading to hypokalemia.

Present-day medicine is paying great attention to the important role which potassium plays in diseases caused by the derangement of the metabolic system.

For example, a recent clinical study reports that a patient with myocardial trouble became better on administration of potassium despite the fact that no effect had been obtained upon the administration of digitalis, a strong cardiotonic.

Edema may occur in heart or renal diseases, and diuretics are often used for the treatment of such edematogenic diseases. These are drugs for increasing the excretion of urine. Furthermore, steroids are used preferentially against various inflammatory diseases. These adrenocortical hormone preparations, drugs of the cortisone type, are also used against pains, infantile asthma and allergic diseases. These agents can temporarily remove inflammation or pains, but their use has recently posed a serious problem. It has been discovered that when a diuretic or a drug of the cortisone type is used, the excretion of potassium from the body fluids abruptly increases.

Physicians continue to use these drugs even though their patients maintain life with difficulty because of a decrease of potassium in the blood. Even while the drug is being administered, there is every possibility that a transitory consumption of great quantities of potassium will occur. This is a very dangerous phenomenon.

When such a therapy is practiced, potassium in a completely natural form should be supplied at the same time. Green Barley Essence, which contains much potassium, works effectively to remove this inconsistency.

Case Studies in Which Potassium Was More Effective Than Cardiac Drugs

It has already been pointed out that various heart diseases are caused by mental stress, unbalanced nutrition or an excessive intake of acidic foods containing fats.

Myocardial infarction, the final form of heart disease, is caused by the clogging of the coronary artery by waste matter. Green Barley Essence acts to promote the decomposition of this waste matter.

Our heart and blood vessels continue to contract and relax from birth to death without a moment's rest. As previously stated, the motion of muscles involves a release of potassium. What happens if potassium is not supplied sufficiently for the working of your heart and blood vessels?

The muscles strongly resist releasing potassium, and if the potassium deficiency is exacerbated by continued consumption of acidic foods containing much fat but few minerals, cholesterol and wastes build up in the blood vessels.

Heart diseases of the middle- and old-aged, such as myocardial infarction, mostly afflict those who eat luxuriously and seem to be exposed to much stress. What is worse, stress also involves a release of potassium.

Green Barley Essence removes these conditions and so serves to prevent heart diseases.

Green Barley Essence, by strengthening muscular power, is also effective for persons who actually have heart diseases. Experiments by the staff of the Medical Department of Keio University have shown that the administration of potassium contained in great quantities in Green Barley Essence was effective against myocardial disorders. They found that myocardial patients showed no effect when given digitalis, but were restored to a nearly normal state when the digitalis was replaced by potassium.

Prevents Cholesterol Deposition

Hypertension and hypotension, also directly related to heart disease, are ascribable to various causes. One of the typical causes of hypertension is the deposition of cholesterol on the walls of the blood vessels. Since cholesterol is produced by an excessive ingestion of fats, the intake of Green Barley Essence has a preventive effect against it. Furthermore, Green Barley Essence can assist in the prevention of the deposition of cholesterol in the blood vessels.

Hypertensive persons are associated with a symptom described as a feeling of swelling in the abdomen. Green Barley Essence enhances the peristalsis of the intestines, relieving constipation. As a result, the waste material which caused the swollen feeling of the abdomen is excreted from the intestinal tract. When by-products of abnormal fermentation in the intestinal tract are absorbed in the blood vessels, they greatly weaken the walls of the blood vessels, especially the capillary vessels. Improvement of evacuation can remove this undesirable activity.

Also, diverticulitis and other forms of colon distress have been reported to be relieved by the introduction of Green Barley Essence directly into the colon through colonic treatment.

Rate of Acquiring Hypertension Is Proportional to the Amount of Sodium Chloride Consumed

The amounts of sodium and potassium ingested must be taken up again in considering hypertension of the Japanese. This can be boiled down to a problem of sodium taken in the form of sodium chloride and potassium ingested from vegetables.

There are many hypertensive patients among Japanese people, who ingest a large quantity of salt from various favorite dishes.

The world survey of the amount of salt consumption per day shows the following result:

Eskimos . . . . 4 g
Marshall Islands 7g
U.S.A. (white) 10g
Farming area in the southern part of Japan 14g
Farming area in the northern part of Japan 26.3g

The incidence of hypertension shows a straight-line increase ranging from 0 for the Eskimos to 39 percent in the farming area in the northern part of Japan. This means that the number of hypertensive patients increases in proportion to the amount of salt taken.

Now, remember the difference in the rate of occurrence of hypertension and cerebral hemorrhage between the farming area of Akita Prefecture and Aomori Prefecture that I cited earlier in this chapter. The lower rate in Aomori Prefecture was due to the potassium in apples, but it is significant that the amount of salt consumed was lower. This is based on a report of Professor Naosuke Sasaki of the Medical Faculty of Hirosaki University.

Since people in Aomori Prefecture took sufficient potassium and less sodium chloride, it is natural that the rate of occurrence of hypertension is low.

Professor Sasaki pointed out that "Hypertension is a disease which mankind has created as a result of such imbalance of diet."

In view of this, it is believed that the only physical way to cure hypertension is to reduce the intake of sodium and to replenish potassium in the body. Potassium chloride is used commonly to treat hypertension, but this induces ulcers within the intestines, and potassium so administered has difficulty entering the cells. The best treatment is the natural ingestion of potassium in natural foods.

Care must be taken in eating canned foods and refrigerated foods, in which, compared with raw foods, the potassium content decreases to half, and the content of sodium increases by 10 to 30 times.

Renal Diseases Are Difficult to Cure by Drugs

Abnormality of the metabolic function can also lead to a kidney condition called nephrosis. Nephrosis is not a single disease, but is the diagnosis when a combination of the four following symptoms appear:

1) Protein in urine increases (amounting to more than 3.5g per day);
2) Protein in the blood decreases;
3) Fats in the blood increase;
4) Edema appears in the body.

Frequently, nephrosis occurs in conjunction with diabetes or arteriosclerosis. Unlike diseases caused by bacterial infection, nephrosis is caused by aggravation of the metabolic function of the whole body, especially the renal function. Hence there is no specific effective therapy except rest and high-protein diet.

When the symptoms of edema or ascites are strong, the patient loses appetite and stops eating adequately at meals. Consequently protein in the blood further decreases. To put an end to this vicious cycle, diuretics such as thiazides are used to temporarily pick up the metabolic function. This is considered only a short-term remedy.

The Fundamental Cure Is to Render the Metabolic Activity within the Body Normal

Diseases of this kind are never completely cured by one cycle of treatment, but are followed by relapses. As diuretics are repeatedly called upon to treat the symptoms, the underlying disease inevitably grows worse because the metabolic function loses its own ability to cure the condition by itself.

There is no fundamental cure for nephrosis and other diseases induced by abnormal metabolism. The only way is to put right the metabolism of the body. Green Barley Essence performs a beneficial function as an auxiliary food that promotes good metabolism. Since Green Barley Essence contains abundant protein, it is also effective as a part of the high-protein diet recommended for victims of nephrosis. Furthermore, the enzymes in it also help break up the increased fats in the blood.

Pancreatitis

Very few curative methods exist for pancreatitis. I was therefore both surprised and pleased to discover that Green Barley Essence produces outstanding results against that disease as well as gastritis and peptic ulcers.

I have already shown how chlorophyll has a wonderful effect against injuries and inflammations. I once cured a heavy skin inflammation caused by scalding water merely by applying juice of green barley.

Chlorophyll works equally well against inflammation of the internal organs and on peptic ulcers and gastritis. I tried this on an acquaintance of mine who had long suffered from gastritis and was taking shots of an analgesic called Buscopan without success. The pain and nausea caused by the woman's gastritis diminished after her first cup of Green Barley Essence dissolved in water. Within a week her gastritis was cured. To those who devote themselves to a study of medicine for the diseased, nothing is more impressive than seeing the pain of the patient relieved before their eyes. With a certain surprise and pride, I then recommended Green Barley Essence to several others who suffered from the same disease. In all cases, the effect was strong.

I immediately asked Professor Toshitsugu Oda, now Director of Tokyo University Hospital, to perform a clinical test of Green Barley Essence.

He agreed and ran a two-year investigation beginning in 1971 on patients who had repeated occurrence of pain from chronic pancreatitis. The investigation was undertaken by Akira Yoshida and Osamu Yokono of the First Internal Medicine Department, Tokyo University Hospital.

The test subjects were selected from the following groups:

1) Patients who experienced repeated occurrence of pain because of chronic repetitive pancreatitis;

2) Patients who felt pressing pain at the pancreas while undergoing X-rays of the digestive tract using an opaque agent;
3) Patients whose urinary amylase values measured very high in more than seven out of ten tests;
4) Patients with pancreas hypertrophy.

The patients so selected were treated with Green Barley Essence and Cospanon, an anticholinergic drug. In many cases, within several days after administration, the symptoms disappeared, the pains were removed, or the intervals between pain recurrence were prolonged. Only 25 percent showed no improvement. The results were also excellent with regard to side effects. The report said that soft feces were observed in only a few patients.

These findings give me great confidence in suggesting that Green Barley Essence should be considered the remedy of choice against such troubles.

Promotes Normal Secretion of Gastric Juice

Gastric troubles account for about 20 percent of all diseases in Japan. Gastritis and gastroptosis are especially common.

Gastritis is a disease caused by abnormal secretion of the gastric juices, resulting in symptoms of hyperacidity, hypoacidity, or anacidity. The hypoacidity tends to follow the ingestion of liquors, cigarettes, and coffee. These habits must be curbed to effect a cure. Mental tension and stress also constitute a great cause of gastritis. For this reason people who constantly work under mental stress frequently develop gastric troubles.

In many cases, this hyperacidity or anacidity, if left untreated, develops into duodenal ulcer or peptic ulcer.

Since the mental tension or stress involves potassium release, Green Barley Essence can counteract the effect by replenishing potassium. At the same time, it promotes normal secretion of gastric juices.

The problem of anacidity, which seems to be on the increase, is worse than that of hyperacidity. Not only does it induce inflammations in various organs, such as cholecystitis and pancreatitis, but it was also found to have some connection with cancer.

Minerals, Enzymes, and Chlorophyll Act in Combination on the Stomach and Intestines

The hyperacidic condition causes an extreme reduction in appetite and sometimes involves diarrhea and headache. Since Green Barley Essence returns the activities of the stomach and intestines to normal and improves digestion, appetite can be regained and the symptoms can be reversed within a fairly short period of time.

Whenever you feel that your stomach is in bad condition, you should take Green Barley Essence as soon as possible. The minerals in it will correct the imbalance within the cells caused by mental tension or stress, and the enzymes will restore functions to normal. When inflammation occurs, the chlorophyll in Green Barley Essence will exhibit its anti-inflammatory activity.

Gastroptosis is very frequently found in women, due to a tendency to weakness of the abdominal muscles. A therapy in wide use involves physically holding in the stomach with a band. But if the abdominal muscles are strengthened, any type of gastroptosis will surely be cured.

As previously stated, a large amount of potassium is

required for the motion of muscles. Therefore, in order to strengthen the muscles, it is all-important to supply minerals, especially potassium. It is only after this that physical exercise for increasing the power of muscles becomes possible. In this sense, too, minerals contained in Green Barley Essence are directly associated with the curing of gastroptosis.

Cirrhosis Hepatitis

To me, the greatest organ in the body is the liver. It performs more than 500 types of activities, examples of which include promotion of digestion, storing of nutrients, and detoxification of toxic substances or fatigue toxins. For this reason, the liver is very hardy, and even when exposed to abuse does not readily develop perceptible symptoms of trouble. It often happens that when one notices a disorder of the liver it is too late to do anything about it. In addition, there are no special curing agents, and this makes liver ailments all the worse.

Without realizing it, many people develop fat deposits in the liver. After a long time, this condition is likely to develop into cirrhosis hepatitis.

A substance called choline has been shown effective in preventing the deposition of fat in the liver, and cholinergic agents have recently become commercially available. But Green Barley Essence contains abundant choline.

Administration of Potassium Saved Patients in Hepatic Coma

Obituaries in newspapers report many deaths caused by cirrhosis hepatitis.

It is said that cirrhosis hepatitis is intrinsically a disease which involves a loss of potassium. Since diuretics and steroids are used for its treatment, all the more potassium is lost. A serious case of hypokalemia may result in hepatic coma, which occurs when the liver stops working completely.

When this condition lasts, the patient loses consciousness, since the brain receives its energy from the glucose sent to the blood after decomposition by the liver. A clinical experiment has shown that administration of potassium to a patient in a hepatic coma can improve the condition, as shown by an electrocardiogram.

To cure liver diseases, I would recommend an essence of corbicula *(Corbicula atrata)*, a kind of freshwater shellfish, together with Green Barley Essence. From ancient times, corbicula has been one of the folk remedies for liver troubles in Japan. For example, when a person infected by jaundice and developing a yellow appearance of the eyes took the corbicula essence, the yellow appearance vanished gradually. An animal experiment, too, has shown that a combination of Green Barley Essence and the corbicula essence has the ability to decompose and excrete fats from within the liver cells.

Furthermore, this combination contains large quantities of organic acids, which play a role in fatigue recovery of the cellular tissues. They also contain much glycogen, which becomes an energy source for the liver.

Supplying Minerals and Vitamins Is a Good Measure for Preventing Neurosis

Modern society is full of stresses which seem to contribute to an increase of hysteria and neuroses, and also of horrible crimes associated with these disorders. I heard that in the United States, about 1.7 million serious crimes are committed per year. The situation is not much different in Japan.

Even if such mental disorders do not directly lead to crimes, almost all of us living in the present age are exhausted and unstable both mentally and emotionally.

Mental and bodily exhaustion stimulates our pituitary gland and adrenal cortex and promotes the secretion of hormones. This is a defense mechanism of the living body, enabling it to cope with changes in its environment. As a result of the excitation of hormonal metabolism, minerals such as potassium, calcium, and magnesium and vitamins within the cells are abnormally consumed and excreted. If these consumed minerals and vitamins are not sufficiently replenished, the stress increases further, and accordingly, more minerals and vitamins are consumed. A vicious cycle is established.

Tranquilizers such as Atraxin are widely taken for symptoms of mental illness. This is a kind of sleeping pill, and cannot be used without a physician's prescription. Long-term use of Atraxin causes such side effects as reduced appetite, which might cause secondary stress.

Green Barley Essence is an ideal alternative. As a natural food, it relieves you of the environmental stresses, stabilizes your mentality and reduces the tendency toward neurosis.

Suppresses Cancerous Cells

In the course of my work on Green Barley Essence, I believe I have established that it has the effect of suppressing cancerous cells. I produced mice infected with cancer by inoculating cancerous cells into the abdomen of mice of a special type, and then divided them into a group given the components of Green Barley Essence and another group not given the Essence. A surprising curative effect was noted in the group given Green Barley Essence. Efforts were then made to determine what component of the Essence had an anti-cancer activity. These efforts led to the discovery that a water-soluble protein portion containing the enzyme SOD had the effect of suppressing cancerous cells. I read a paper on this study to a conference of a professional society in 1978.

SOD Is Particularly Effective Against Leukemia and Diffusion Collagen Disease

Elsewhere, the study into the causes and possible treatments of cancer has also turned up considerable evidence of the influence of enzymes, particularly SOD.

Cancer results from the sudden uncontrolled division and growth of cells using the neighboring cells as nutrients. It can be hypothesized that a naturally existing enzyme may act to inhibit the division and growth of cancerous cells. This theory was advanced in a report by Dr. Kazue Sato, Head of the Radiotherapeutic Divison, Takasaki National Hospital, Japan, published at the 34th Conference of the Japanese Association of Oncology.

Dr. Sato stated: "Man has the ability to form an antibody which excludes or inhibits a foreign matter that has come into the body. In order to exhibit this ability, man has a mechanism of watching and defending cells by which the invasion of an antigen is immediately noticed. The occurence of cancer is due presumably to the disordering of this defending mechanism."

Based on this hypothesis, he used enzymes to improve the watching and defending mechanism of the patients. He obtained good results, as evidenced by the fact that of all clinical examples examined, only 3.1 percent were ineffective.

A striking effect of SOD was reported in the United States after it was clinically applied to patients with cancer in order to prevent side effects in radiotherapy.

In 1976, Takashi Sugimura, Manager of the National Cancer Research Institute, found that the charred residue of fish contains a strong carcinogenic substance, and named it Try-P_1 and Try-P_2. This substance is said to have 10 to 20 thousand times as much carcinogenicity as the benzopyrene contained in tobacco.

Thus it was found that the burning residues of fish or meat we eat every day contain a carcinogenic substance. Later, it was found that when various amino acids are burned, the same mutagenic substance forms. The carcinogenic substance Try-P_1 and Try-P_2 causes a change in a human gene DNA, and acts as a trigger for its growth into cancer cells.

I have discovered in Green Barley Essence an enzyme which renders this carcinogenic substance nonhazardous. This enzyme is a heme protein. In 1979, we succeeded in extracting the heme protein, and reported this development in a meeting of the Japanese Society of Pharmaceutical Science. This caused a great sensation.

Professor Takekazu Horio commented: "The result is indeed clear. Separation and purification to that extent is an astonishing success. Among mutagenic substances, Try-P_1 and Try-P_2 has by far the strongest mutagenicity. Green Barley Essence has the ability to attack a substance having such powerful mutagenicity."

Catalase, a Key to Solve the Secret of Cancer

I have already described the importance of the enzyme called SOD in the prevention and treatment of cancer. Another potential therapy for cancer involves use of a respiratory enzyme called catalase.

This enzyme performs an oxidation-reduction activity within the cells. During the course of respiration, the cells produce hydrogen peroxide (H_2O_2) as a by-product. Hydrogen peroxide has the property of coagulating proteins, and is frequently used as a disinfectant. But within the body it is a toxic substance which attacks the cells.

Catalase decomposes toxic hydrogen peroxide into water and oxygen. Healthy cells necessarily contain catalase. But cancerous cells have been found to contain too little catalase. Unlike normal cells, the cancerous cells are anaerobic, meaning they do not respire oxygen in the air or transported through the blood. Instead, they gain the energy they need to metabolize within their own cells. In addition, while normal cells spread, divide and grow or age and die, the cancerous cells do nothing but grow. Since the cancer cells have such a special energy metabolism function, they do not require catalase.

The X-ray radiation frequently used for cancer therapy utilizes this property. When the human body is exposed to X-rays, hydrogen peroxide is generated. With healthy cells, catalase acts immediately to decompose it into water and oxygen.

However, the cancerous cells, which possess hardly any catalase, cannot decompose the hydrogen peroxide but are destroyed.

Iron and Copper Ions in Green Barley Essence Produce Anticarcinogenic Substances

In connection with the relation between catalase and

cancerous cells, I wish to cite an interesting work which suggests the importance of diet. It involves milk, which is certainly one of our most popular foods.

An experimental report suggests that milk may reduce catalase activity in the body fluids. When experimental rats were fed on a diet high in cow's milk, an apparent loss of catalase activity was observed. This would lead to a rise in hydrogen peroxide in the course of metabolism, adversely affecting the cells.

Another experimental report showed that a milk-containing meal also decreased the level of cytochrome oxidase, which is also an important respiratory enzyme.

These reactions are said to occur because of the reduction in iron and copper ions. Catalase is an enzyme having an iron ion, and cytochrome oxidase contains both an iron ion and a copper ion. In other words, these enzymes cannot be formed unless there are plenty of iron and copper ions in the blood.

As shown in Figure 6, milk has a low content of copper and iron. This is not only the case with milk, but also with butter, polished rice and bleached bread. Too much of these foods can weaken the activities of the important enzymes in our body, resulting in cancer. I conjecture that a key to the inhibition of cancer might be hidden here.

Green Barley Essence—a Diet to Prevent Cancer

About two years ago, I extracted a specific component from Green Barley Essence and requested the Cancer Chemotherapy Center at Otsuka, Tokyo to test it for its anticarcinogenic activity. The results indicated a clear inhibitory effect on certain kinds of cancerous cells. However, when the component was purified, there was no effect. The reason for this is still not known,

FIGURE 6
Comparison of the Iron and Copper Content of Green Barley
Essence and Several Foods by Weight (Milligrams per 100 Grams)

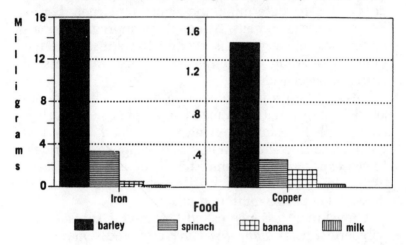

Food Key and Data

Iron		Copper	
1. **Green Barley Essence**	15.8	1. **Green Barley Essence**	1.36
2. Spinach	3.3	2. Spinach	.26
3. Banana	.4	3. Banana	.16
4. Milk	.1	4. Milk	.02

but I presume that what was effective against the cancer was not a pure substance but the organic action of
various components in Green Barley Essence. There
are several candidates which I am still studying.

One is a group of substances called mucopolysaccharides, which are attracting worldwide attention as possi-
bly valuable in the immunological treatment of cancer.

When I had the opportunity to speak about Green
Barley Essence with the late Dr. Tomizo Yoshida,
then Manager of the Japan Cancer Institute, he showed

a great interest in the fact that it is a green juice extract of the leaves of barley. At my request he agreed to conduct an experiment at the Cancer Chemotherapeutic Center to determine the effect of Green Barley Essence on cancer cells. Although no appreciable pharmacological effect was observed in these tests, the Essence was found to contain very large amounts of mucopolysaccharides.

I have noted a folk remedy in which Coix lacryma-jobi Kinne, a variation of ma-yuen Stapf or pearl barley, is very effective for removing warts. Pearl barley is a graminaceous plant abundant in mucopolysaccharides. In an experiment I administered an extract of pearl barley to mice infected by Ehrlich ascites tumor. It showed a superior inhibiting effect.

A mushroom essence called Cortinellus shiitake and polypore *(Fomes glaucotus)* have attracted some attention as anticarcinogenic foods because they contain mucopolysaccharides. Bamboo grass was also reputed as an anticarcinogenic agent because of its mucopolysaccharide content.

Generally, mucopolysaccharides are found in large quantities in graminaceous plants. It has been confirmed that Green Barley Essence contains them in still larger amounts. A description of specific curative effects must await more clinical experiments to be made in the future, but it surely can be expected to have anticarcinogenic activity.

I believe that one method of preventing cancer is to increase green substantially in our diet. Green Barley Essence contains active natural enzymes in sufficient amounts as well as catalase and cytochrome oxidase.

I do not say that Green Barley Essence is the only ideal diet, but it seems that our habit is to underuse green in our meals. We tend to feel at ease by taking milk and eggs, thinking that they provide enough nutrition. We are too much affected by dietetic promotion of proteins and calories—we should not forget that good nutrition is a balanced combination of nutrients.

Repairs DNA Subjected to Mutation

Recently, more news on cancer came from Dr. Ames of the United States, a Nobel Laureate, who discovered a simple method for testing a carcinogenic substance. This method is intended to discover a mutagenic substance by using microorganisms of the genus Salmonella. Medicines, chemical substances, food additives, agricultural chemicals, environmental pollutants, automotive exhaust gases, etc. have been tested by the Ames method, and many carcinogenic substances have been discovered. Specifically, several thousand carcinogenic substances have been found in many chemical agents we are exposed to every day. Further investigations have shown that about 80 percent of these carcinogenic substances are nitrogen oxide derivatives.

Seeing this, I ran experiments to determine whether Green Barley Essence would be effective against these carcinogenic nitrogen oxides, and ascertained that it is.

In April 1981, Dr. Hotta, a biochemist and a professor at the University of California, and I read the results of this joint work at a meeting of the Japanese Society of Pharmaceutical Science. The work was an epochal one and consisted of restoring a DNA gene infected by cancer to a normal condition by application of the components of a juice taken from the young leaves of barley. This received front-page coverage in the leading Japanese newspapers, *Yomiuri Shimbun* and *Mainichi Shimbun*.

These carcinogenic nitrogen oxides are present in

many foodstuffs we eat every day. These are air pollutants or products of petroleum decomposition. They dissolve in water and foodstuffs, and come into our body. They are compounds bearing the prefix nitro-, such as nitrobenzene and nitrophenol. In particular, 4-nitroquinoline oxide (4NQO) is known as a strong carcinogenic substance.

We are living amidst a flood of these carcinogenic substances. We can reduce their danger to us by making a regular habit of taking Green Barley Essence for our self-defense.

In truth, any green raw vegetable would do. But components of heated vegetables have no power to render these substances nontoxic.

It has been found that Green Barley Essence contains an abundance of enzymes and lecithin-like substances, and these perform complex activities and repair and restore DNA subjected to mutation by X-rays or environmental pollutants to its normal condition.

CHAPTER 8 ════════════════

THE FUTURE OF GREEN BARLEY ESSENCE

INVITATION FOR WORLDWIDE RESEARCH

WE HAVE SEEN a number of the pharmacological effects of Green Barley Essence, and in this connection I wish to give a brief account of how I came to found the Association of Green and Health.

In the present day, people all over the world are compelled to live in polluted environments. Industrial pollutants such as PCB (polychlorinated biphenyl) and mercury can be detected from the ice in the Antarctic and Arctic Zones. Agricultural chemicals are even affecting maternal milk. In addition, all processed food products contain synthetic food additives.

As I said before, I once believed that only the development of science and technology would be the way to save the confusion of Japan after World War II, as most Japanese also believed. I devoted myself ardently to a study of various synthetic pharmaceuticals, including a drug for athlete's foot, hair-nourishing preparations and cosmetics.

Since I paid a severe price for submerging myself in the pollution caused by the new synthetic drugs, I cannot be indifferent to the present unfortunate situation.

We cannot but doubt whether science will be able to save mankind.

There are many problems with the present system of medical therapy. Many hospitals are urged to study the cure of diseases only at the expense of paying attention to their prevention. The general practicing physician can do nothing but try to cure diseases. Whether shortage of budget or manpower is the cause, preventive medicine, the need for which every person engaged in medicine keenly feels, is neglected.

The final purpose of medicine should be to prevent mankind from diseases and to promote sound body and mentality.

This was the motive which spurred my interest in a study of Chinese herb drugs. During the course of this study I discovered Green Barley Essence. When I discovered through analysis the surprisingly large quantities of active ingredients of Green Barley Essence, I thought it was a revelation from the heavens.

I came to believe that if we could receive the nutrition of green plants, which produce oxygen as a source of life and which contain minerals, enzymes, chlorophyll and vitamins in great quantities, we could recapture the large-heartedness, strong body and spirit of primitive man. Many people shared my belief, and this led to the foundation of the Association of Green and Health. I earnestly solicit you to join the Association, whose only code is: "Partake abundantly of vegetables having deep green colors."

For details, write to, or call, the Association at the following address: Daido Bldg., Room No. 303, 3-5-5, Uchikanda, Chiyoda-ku, Tokyo, 101, Japan (tel. 03-256-8106).

The Hagiwara Institute of Health: Research Continues

Now I have told you what I know about Green Barley Essence and its benefits to the health of mankind. That knowledge is based on my own intuition, the testimony of those who have tried Green Barley Essence, technical evaluations coming from my studies and the research being done by scientists around the world.

Though I believe the information presented here gives us a good basis for concluding that Green Barley Essence has extraordinary value in the prevention and cure of many of man's common ailments, I must admit that we are still far from knowing all the answers.

For one thing, we still don't have a clear idea how toxins are broken down and removed from the body. The study of the specific substances which can cause cancer, and others which suppress cancer, could still be described as an infant endeavor.

As a businessman, I am not compelled to concern myself with these questions. But, it is my hope to conclude my work in this life as more than a businessman. I have been fortunate so far to be able to offer the world a product which has measurably improved the health of many who have received it. My personal effort will not be finished, however, until I have learned everything I can about the mechanisms of good health in the living body.

To help further this knowledge, in 1970 I founded a private research organization called the Hagiwara Institute of Health. For more than a decade, I have used this laboratory to conduct research into products which may prove effective against adult diseases, including cancer and diabetes, and others which may promote longevity.

Just last year I built a new facility for the laboratory

on eight acres near Osaka. I also increased its staff to twenty scientists.

Many distinguished scientists have visited the Hagiwara Institute, including Dr. Mendelssohn from the University of San Diego Cancer Center and Dr. Gordon Sato, a well-known cell biologist.

We would welcome all scientists and researchers in the field of nutrition to visit the Institute, to learn of our work and to make any suggestions that might assist us.

Green Barley Essence Will Avert a Possible Food Crisis

I would like to conclude this book with a look into the future of the food industry. A grim picture it is.

The ruin of mountains and fields and the drastic reductions in the number of green trees as a result of exploitation of agricultural lands for housing present a foreboding picture ahead for a world that is already growing familiar with mass starvation. Many experts predict that the overburdened agricultural system will soon be unable to keep pace with the world's expanding populations. By the year 2000, the population of the world is expected to double, climbing above 8,000 million. If food production cannot be proportionally multiplied, the inevitable result will be a worldwide food crisis.

Shinya Nishimaru, a Japanese dietary ecologist, has said that in order to avoid a food crisis, the world will have to dramatically improve the efficiency of calorie production. Nishimaru warns that if the industrial world continues to rely on beef as its primary source of nutrition, the caloric value of grasses eaten by cows will be denied to other human beings.

The arithmetic of this waste is stunning. To raise one

cow requires all the grass that can grow on ten ares of land, about a quarter of an acre. Let's assume this one cow feeds thirty persons. During the same time that that cow is sustaining those thirty lives, the protein which could be harvested directly from barley leaves grown on that ten ares of land would sustain three hundred lives.

I believe this would be an advantageous measure to counter the expected food crisis.

If we take Green Barley Essence from young barley leaves instead of relying on the conventional practice of breeding and killing animals for flesh, we will be able to harvest several times as much protein, vitamins and minerals as we do today, as well as other nutrients which can help powerfully to maintain the health of mankind.

I can think of no more optimistic thought upon which to conclude this story.